FORCE

MEMORIES OF HARRIS (1955 – 1964)

3h ff Boops. a Beolong.
c. B. B MacLeanan
43 Percival Rd Sth.
Stornoway.

FORCE 12
MEMORIES OF HARRIS (1955 – 1964)

Geoffrey Wilkinson

Ellingham Press

British Library Cataloguing in Publication Data
A catalogue record for this book is available from the British Library

ISBN 978-0-9570781-8-5
Ellingham Press, 43 High Street, Much Wenlock, Shropshire TF13 6AD
Cover design and typesetting: Aardvark Illustration & Design (www.aardvarkid.co.uk)
Printed in Great Britain by Berforts Information Press Ltd

CONTENTS

Dedicated to the Crofters of Harris,
past and present, wonderful characters all.

FOREWORD

IN 1950 I WAS coming towards the end of my first tour in Zanzibar
as an agricultural development officer. It was all right for a quick
holiday, but a very unhealthy climate to be working in for two or
three years non-stop. High temperatures, high humidity, and if you
had forgotten to pump up the tyres of the Land Rover before leaving
home in the morning you had to change shirts before you left because after pumping up one or two tyres to the correct pressure you
had a sweat-sodden shirt. I worked hard, developing a 100-acre research station from scratch some twenty miles away from Zanzibar
town on the east coast, and often played hard, going into Zanzibar
for a game of tennis or taking out a nurse for the evening. This
lifestyle for a 24-year-old invited every tropical disease under the
sun, and not surprisingly I finally contracted encephalitis which put
me in hospital for a month. My left side was paralysed and caused
the government to send a cable home saying they did not expect me
to live. However, luck was on my side and I survived, and two or
three months before my official leave was due they sent me home to
Britain to have some sick leave back in the UK in an equable climate.

So I flew to the Kenyan port of Mombasa and joined the SS
Mantola (British India Line), and waited in the port for the Kenyan
passengers to join the ship. On the first night out from Mombasa
there was a bit of a dance on deck and I noticed a strawberry blonde
with huge blue eyes wearing a navy-blue, polka-dot dress and a pair
of 'Joyce' blue sandals (wedge heels) sitting out with no male in
attendance, so I went up and asked her if she would like a dance and
she agreed. After a dance or two I suggested she come up to the
boat-deck to have a look at the constellations in the African night
sky! Fortunately, the journey took one month, which was ample time
in which to get to know Patricia Entwisle and her father and mother
who were keeping an eye on her, having been out on holiday visiting
friends in Kenya. When we docked at Southampton, we bid each
other goodbye, not knowing whether we would meet again.

Pat disappeared to the Outer Hebrides to visit her aunt and uncle who lived on the Isle of Harris, while I disappeared into the University College Hospital in London to be sorted out medically. We kept in touch and two months later I was invited to go and stay at Pat's house, which was fatal. I had six months' home leave and, realising that time was of the essence, we agreed to get married and did so at St Mary's Church, Hitchin in Hertfordshire. For our honeymoon, we went up to the Isle of Harris to stay at the Lodge owned by Pat's uncle and aunt. Having learnt how to fly-fish in Kenya, I was soon enjoying the fishings for sea trout and salmon which belonged to the Lodge. In other words, I was 'hooked'!

October came, we had to get on board a ship, in this case the *Dunottar Castle* belonging to the Union Castle Line, and we headed for Zanzibar. Soon after arriving there I was posted to the island of Pemba as the sole agricultural officer in charge of forestry, fisheries and agriculture. We had an idyllic three years there; the only thing we had to attend to of any concern was the mail steamer which came up from Zanzibar once a week. If I did not like the contents of the mail, I would tell my Goan clerk, Albert Martins, to 'WPB' it (wastepaper basket it!) and we would only bother to answer it if the sender wrote again on the same subject, which proved a very efficient method of administration. Further consideration of three years in Zanzibar and three years in Pemba must be reserved for another book because, for many reasons, I was not happy in the Colonial Service and decided to make a complete break. But there was the problem of deciding what to do when one abandoned a free house, a good salary and good home leave. Everybody considered I was an idiot throwing it up and leaving. That was an act of faith or folly.

We arrived back in Britain by boat, bought a Land Rover, bought some furniture at auction rooms in Bognor Regis where landladies were throwing out good, old-fashioned furniture (military chest of drawers, mahogany, brass fittings: £5). We loaded furniture into a trailer and filled the Land Rover as well because this coincided with a telegram from the aunt in the Hebrides, whose husband, now in his early eighties, was very seriously ill, asking if we could go up there and help. So we went up and we didn't come back again. The uncle died in 1954 – he was a super chap. He had served in the regular army as an officer in the Black Watch regiment, first in the Boer War and then as a colonel in the Great War, being awarded the Military Cross.

The Lodge was far too large and run-down as a result of the war for the aunt to manage on her own, so Pat and I bought the Lodge with its attendant 115 acres of land and its salmon and sea trout fishings. The land was one of the few parcels owned by an individual. The rest of the island was largely divided into crofts, small units occupied by individual crofters. Thus began our ten years on Harris.

SOUTH HARRIS

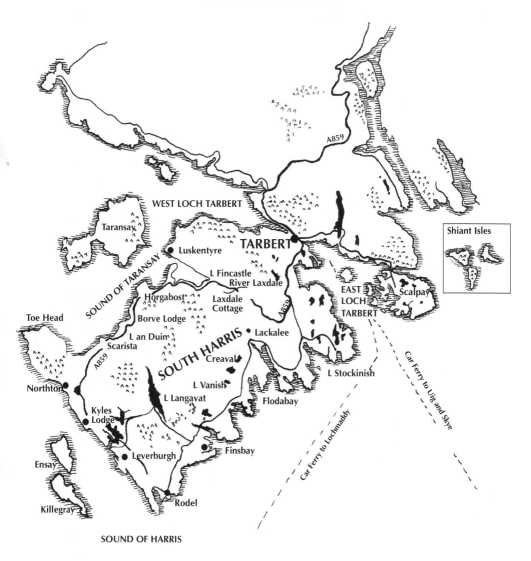

THE EARLY YEARS

WE SPENT a night or two en route and when we got to the final stretch, a single-track highland road with passing places, we catnapped the final night in the Land Rover and next morning we reached Kyle of Lochalsh. There the car was loaded onto the *Loch Mor*, a David MacBrayne steamer. In those days MacBrayne's did not have the luxury of stabilisers and the *Loch Mor* was noted for its ability to corkscrew its way across the Minch, rolling and pitching with equal venom.

On the way over, looking westward, you can see the hills of Harris and the smaller peaks of North Uist, and there is a definite feeling of the Romance of the Isles in the air. Bird-life in the Minch distracted my attention from the rolling and pitching as I watched Gannets and Manx Shearwaters swooping and fishing parallel to the ship. We knew that we were more than halfway across when we passed just to the south of the Shiant Islands, famous for the massive sea bird populations nesting on its steep cliffs.

We were glad to reach the quieter waters of East Loch Tarbert where the way through the rocks is well marked with various marker buoys, finally leading to the head of the loch to Tarbert's small port where the Land Rover was winched ashore in its steel mesh net. Reference to the sketch map will show the road leading out of Tarbert which, in spite of its rather rough condition, took us on its single track to the west coast of Harris.

Halfway there, after much upping and downing over blind hills (a nightmare at night), the vista opens up to give the most glorious view of an estuary with the island of Taransay two miles off the coast. Since the sea bed consists of white shell sand it reflects the blue of the sky, the variety of blues depending on the depth of the water. Going down the hill towards the estuary on the left is the series of lochs which feed the Laxdale river, the final loch being artificial at the head of the estuary.

The main road travels the length of Loch Fincastle and, having stopped to admire the scene, we drove on the west coast road for another five or six miles before seeing the lovely vista of Borve Lodge, our destination, standing a hundred yards from the seashore and the estuary of a small stream. This noble pile had firstly been a shooting and fishing lodge for the Earl of Dunmore, who had extended it, and then finally it was owned by Lord Leverhulme who made yet further alterations and additions. He finished his days in a wheel-chair there, and so his workers levelled out a sand dune to enable his chair to be pushed on the flat to get a full view of the sea.

The Lodge was owned by Colonel Walker and his wife Kathleen, Pat's aunt (known as Dick), and for economy's sake they had lived throughout the war in a nearby cosy cottage belonging to the Lodge. They had now moved back into the Lodge which had a magical air about it, helped by the fact that it was run down. The walls were cov-ered in ivy which had eaten into the harling (pebbledashing), the windows were beginning to rot and all needed paint, some slates were missing off the roof, the boiler room below ground was com-pletely flooded to soil level – there was no heating and no lighting because there was no electricity. A candle could easily blow out on the way upstairs to bed!

The front porch led into a hall which was notable for the pair of scales used for weighing fish. All catches of fish were carefully recorded in a game book, and indeed for the 'caught on flies' only, the annual catch was about 22 salmon and 84 sea trout, the salmon weighing an average of five to six pounds and the sea trout averaging about a pound and a half. The only other item of note was the dial barometer hanging in the hall. As the old fisherman said to the young lad, who was also staying at the Lodge and who was banging on the barometer, 'Young man, if you were meant to bang the baro-meter like that a hammer would have been provided.'

Borve Lodge in 1900 before new north wing was built.

The hall gave way to an impressive staircase which led up to a corridor which was beautifully lined with large-scale maps of the whole area at six inches to the mile, so on a wet day visitors could usefully spend time studying the maps. The corridor led through to what was 'Lord Leverhulme's sanctum', a vast sitting-room with windows on three sides and a double bedroom off one end of it. The whole room was lined on the blank inner wall with superb hardwood cupboards which would delight any squirrelling female (this includes my good wife)! The floor was covered in a lovely short-pile, forest-green carpet, with two or three bedrooms off the top landing and a further four bedrooms on the ground floor. This we called Wing No. 1. The construction was of the highest quality.

Returning to the entrance hall, another door led off into the dining-room with an adjacent kitchen which had an ancient but excellent Aga. A second staircase that led to four bedrooms constituted Wing No. 2.

Finally from the kitchen a further small staircase led to the three servants' bedrooms. Colonel Walker was sufficiently well off to employ a wonderful housemaid and cook called Mary MacKay. I suppose you would call them in those days a 'cook general' and 'Wee' Mary, to assist as a kitchen youngster and general hand.

Borve Lodge in 1960. West and south face with outbuildings converted to new byre and loose boxes.

There were numerous outbuildings which included a very large garage with further bedrooms above it. Another building housed the fish hatchery and a generator room for a now defunct electrical generating system, a cool dairy (for there was a butter churn for churning home-produced cream into butter) and cool storage for meat and fish. There was no electricity for refrigerators and no paraffin refrigerators.

Borve Lodge in 1955. East face with round garden in foreground, estuary and the warren in background.

Alongside the dairy was a most beautiful round garden created by Lord Leverhulme, which was surrounded by a circular stone wall about ten feet high and three feet thick, with flower beds formed within it like the spokes of a wheel. The garden ornaments consisted of about ten different figures carved from stone on their individual pedestals set against the wall at intervals around the garden. Finally in the centre was a modern sundial made of bronze which was very accurate in its readings and the time. The main entrance to the garden had a lovely wrought-iron gate which was suffering from the periodic salt spray cover, as the Lodge was only a hundred yards from the seashore. The Lodge would actually shake in a Force 12 westerly gale!

Colonel Walker's first marriage happily produced two sons, Gavin and Ian, but they were both killed in World War II while serving with the RAF. In a way it was merciful that their mother did not live to endure this tragedy, as she died after a long illness during which she was nursed by Kathleen Noar who also looked after the boys. When the colonel's wife died he married 'Dick', so-called because she was always a rugged tomboy type. In the summer they used to let their house and take their Car Cruiser caravan up to Scotland to enjoy rented salmon and trout fishing. On one of their trips they discovered Borve Lodge and bought it together with its excellent sporting. They made it their permanent home from the early thirties.

The loss of Colonel Walker's two sons made him decide to do something to benefit the returning ex-servicemen in Harris and so, using his own capital, he formed the Harris Crofters Association in memory of the two boys. Against the odds, with his headquarters in an ancient, woodworm-ridden farmhouse nearby, he prepared, with crofter staff, the warp and the weft for weavers in Harris and Lewis to weave genuine Harris Tweed which was then mainly exported to America, Australia and New Zealand where commission agents sold it readily for winter wear.

Dick, the colonel's wife, was very keen on weaving and had her own loom, and she would spin her own weft. She wove a lovely piece of brown-patterned tweed from which she had a tailored suit made, or costume as it was called in those days – sadly, that was her *magnum opus*. But, being a squirrel, she retained several sacks of wool which relatives laboriously washed every time they came on holiday and hung it out to dry only to have it bagged again. It was an annual event, this washing of the wool to get the moths out of it on the promise of having lovely tweed made from it. Men and women like that are so creative that they provide a lot of free entertainment for anyone watching.

It is well to explain that in pre-war and immediate post-war times lodges like Borve Lodge, with their attendant sportings, were largely occupied by monied owners with private incomes large enough to ensure that the running costs of such an establishment were comfortably met.

This was the first adjustment that the local crofting population had to make, namely that we were there to make a living and that the sportings were very much of secondary interest, except from the point of view of their careful management and improvement and their letting potential to fishers from the mainland. So it came as a bit of a shock to the crofters to find a very practical couple like us tackling fencing, drainage, digging, vegetable-growing and handling livestock without employing resident keepers and resident labour. So the 100 acres which we took on was rather like an amphitheatre with us living in a goldfish bowl, with every move observed from the hills by every crofter eager to see what these Sassenachs were going to do next. One or two efforts had been made on an adjacent estate in previous years by a retired doctor, Dr Robertson, to farm some land, but with serious losses of livestock, for medical practitioners are not ideal farmers for the Outer Hebrides. Among the locals there were several prophets of doom who said that 'Old Wilkie' would do no better. Indeed, Dick was sceptical about my plans and my ability to make something out of nothing. She had not really bargained for the enormous energy that we possessed, able to exploit the endless daylight hours of May and June for achieving far more work than was normal for the Outer Hebrides.

It was a good thing that we had not produced a fixed plan for how we were going to set about the work of life in Harris and above all making a living. Before arriving in Harris I must admit that I had notions of perhaps starting an enterprise to produce virus-free strawberry plants, blackcurrants, etc. and then running a postal service to the mainland customers, thus cashing in on the fact that it is far too windy in the Western Isles for the aphids vector of virus diseases to exist. However, from the general chaos that abounded both in the house and outbuildings on the 115 acres of land, the quite clear priority was to get the basics in order first before thinking about complex projects. Thus the farming policy, such as it was, was primarily determined by the state of the fencing, which was derelict, the state of the pastures, which were overgrazed by the wild ponies and invading sheep, not to mention the worst pest of all – rabbits. The machair land represented a heavenly habitat for rabbits, sandy soil in which to dig burrows and provide short, sweet grazing.

So the early activity on the farm was the renovation of the boundary fencing. This included perfecting an imitation sheepdog whistle, which was soon taken up by the resident starlings, so if a raiding sheep was up on the hill and had broken through the boundary fence, all I had to do was blow this piercing whistle as if I was handling a sheepdog and the sheep would run away for its life, breaking back out of the dilapidated fencing. This even worked with the local starlings singing from the roof top as they copied my whistle and sent sheep packing! Talking of calls, I am reminded that when I began to get cattle, I trained them to get accustomed to my call so that if they were way up on the hill and I wanted to handle them I could call them down without having to climb 500 feet up the hill to get them. From my early days working on a farm before going to college I had developed a cattle call – 'koo-op', 'koo-op', 'koo-op', 'koo-op' – always when I wanted to give them an extra feed or something of that nature I trained them to come to that call. The only snag was that the neighbouring crofters thought I was alerting them to the arrival of the Co-operative travelling grocer's van and they would rush out with their baskets and purses to get their weekly orders. How difficult it was for the crofters to accommodate a mad young Englishman!

1955 – Shetland ponies and miscellaneous sheep on unimproved pasture in the park.

The sketch map *(inside the back cover)* gives a view of the farm from the sea and really the farm was divided into three sections. Firstly, the sandy machair on which the Lodge stood; behind was the peat section, and behind that the hill. More or less in front of the Lodge and about 150 yards away was a little bay which I christened Seal Bay because in the autumn one year a young seal which had drowned was washed up in the bay. It was a young Atlantic seal, the grey seal, which had been born to the westward on the island of Shillay. Gales and a very rough sea had washed it off the flat rocks where it was born and it ended up three miles to the east in Seal Bay at Borve. Another interesting rarity that was washed up at

Seal Bay was a Little Auk, quite a rare seabird, not very often seen – it was dead, of course, and had been washed up in the little bay. The grey seals live and mate in quite large numbers in the islands and were the source of a modest number of seal skins which Donald MacLeod turned into sporrans and purses as part of his living producing country crafts.

The shell sand which made up the machair, with its wonderful array of wild flowers, was stabilised by a band of marram grass. We were lucky that between the main road and the sea we had a freshwater loch, Loch Cistavat. This provided good, fresh drinking water for livestock grazing in that area of the Warren (it was called the 'Warren' because of the number of rabbits there) together with a small gathering of cattle that used to wander over daily from Horgabost common grazing. Thus, when I came to renew the fencing along the roadside, I created a special corridor to enable the Horgabost cattle to come down off the road to drink at Cistavat so I did not infringe on the habitual provision of water for local cattle.

Cistavat had its own stock of Loch Leven trout which attracted the occasional otter that could be viewed from the higher position of the main road swimming underwater and fishing as it went. It was a favoured bathing place for seagulls which would enjoy bathing in the fresh water as they got rid of the salt out of their feathers. It was also a favoured patch for the whooper swans when they came down from Iceland to winter in the Hebrides. Being creatures of habit, one family was particularly fond of spending the winter on Loch Cistavat. Its waters were shallow enough to enable swans with their long-reach necks to feed on the plentiful vegetation that was growing in the loch. It was lovely to hear their honking as they talked to each other as a family, and having come down from Iceland in October they would get restless when the spring came and join up with big flocks of whooper swans and geese going back to Iceland to nest in the spring. (See my booklet *A Bird Watcher in the Isle of Harris*.)

The east bank of the loch went up quite steeply to the road, and the rocky outcrops and black soil were covered in heather. This seemed to thrive on the salt spray driven in by westerly gales, perhaps making the heather more appetising for livestock to browse on.

Splitting the machair into two halves, the stream that came down from the hills gouged out a sea pool just below the road bridge and then carried on into its own mini-estuary into the sea. Later on this proved to be a very good source of drinking water for the cattle which were turned out throughout the winter – to go down to the sea pool and the estuary to drink.

Standing on the road bridge looking down on the sea pool, a half-buried sheet of corrugated-iron was visible in the sandy bottom and a good sea trout seemed very happy to make that its base there. If anybody tried to catch it, it would shoot under the sheet of corrugated-iron, thus cutting the fisherman's cast.

We used to let out the bedroom and large sitting-room forming Lord Leverhulme's old sanctum early in the season to fishermen. A QC, Sir Lionel Heald, and his son Anthony rented it for two weeks at the beginning of one fishing season. On a pouring wet day they sat in the big sitting-room overlooking the sea pool when Sir Lionel spotted this good sea trout leap out of the water and so the hue and cry went up: 'Anthony, Anthony, bring my rods.' So Anthony, who was about 21 years old at the time, hastened to gather up his two rods, and well wrapped up against the wind and the rain they went down to the burn and took up a position under the bridge, floating their flies downstream with the current – one by one the fish took the flies and the lines got cut on the edge of the corrugated-iron when the fish dashed for the shelter of its home. Poor Sir Lionel – after a morning of hard endeavour and having lost a number of good flies, they gave up the struggle and came back, suitably soaked by the heavy rain, bringing their rods but no fish. Thereafter we christened the fish 'Sir Lionel' and it went on to survive many attempts to catch it!

Sir Lionel was an eminent Queen's Counsel frequently representing large companies in court in their fight for justice. In this case, he had just successfully defended BP against charges arising over a BP tanker that was anchored in the harbour at Cardiff and although it was empty, it had exploded causing a lot of damage to the harbour works. There is nothing like fishing for being a leveller!

The little estuary after a westerly gale was a wonderful source of bladderwrack seaweed which I would collect with a tractor and trailer. The second important section of the farm, on the rising ground, was a peaty subsoil which started as a thin layer of sand overlying peat and then, heading inland, formed a deep peat bog in which a number of the Shetland ponies had died by drowning. At really high tides, the salt water would go up the estuary and up the burn to almost the extremity of the peat bog before giving way to much higher ground. This ground was very rocky, covered in heather and coarse grasses. It led to Borve Loch, being a useful loch for occasional fishing for sea trout which had run on a spate from the sea, up to feed in the loch which, with its shallow banks and shore, was a good drinking place for livestock.

Borve Loch at top end the of the park with Bleaval in the distance.

Lord Dunmore, when he lived in Borve Lodge, was determined to plant a few trees, so on the flanks of the valley above the peaty area he planted a shelter belt of *Pinus contorta*, a low-growing tree which instead of growing up vertically tended to sprawl and form almost an impenetrable mass – except to a good Labrador who would bravely burrow into it and flush out the Woodcock when they came in during the winter. Beyond the shelter of this *Pinus contorta* Lord Dunmore planted Douglas fir and Sitka spruce which were thus protected from the severe salt spray which used to go up the valley in a cloud during a strong westerly gale.

As you will see from the sketch map, outside the land owned by the Lodge was a large freshwater loch, Loch an Duin, so-called because of the island in the loch with its own little fort (Duin), so it's 'the loch with the fort'. The pipelines with their controlling water cocks were all accurately mapped and the maps made available with the deeds of the Lodge. The boundary ended on the foothill of the hill called Bulaval (1,150 feet high), and a short walk through the gap between Bulaval and the neighbouring Bleaval (1,305 feet high) led to the biggest loch on the island, Loch Langavat. Both Bulaval and Bleaval with their rocky terrain were well clothed in heather which provided good cover for the Red Grouse feeding almost entirely on the bell-heather *(Erica tetralix)* and to a lesser extent on the more common heather *(Calluna vulgaris)*.

Cottage by the gate, the park and Bulaval behind.

Always popular with visitors to the Lodge was the expedition to Bleaval which I conducted for anything up to half a dozen men and their sons on the Glorious Twelfth (12 August) which is a celebrated day – the opening of the grouse-shooting season. We would leave the Lodge after I had held a drill to make sure that everybody was aware of the basic rules of shooting in a group (Mr Pickwick and his party would have benefited from such a drill!). On rising ground above the Lodge was Borve House with a useful area of machair running down from there to the sea. There was a corrugated-iron hut adjacent to the house which would take two or three cattle – this was the only byre available to me – and the ground went on seawards towards the henhouse which was a corrugated-iron shed nearer to the sea. There, half buried in the ground was the silhouette made out of sheet steel of a stag which was used long ago for target practice by guests to the Lodge, who were taken out to stalk the occasional stag on the hill. The population of deer was greatly depleted when the Home Guard was formed during World War II and the members were issued with .303 rifles.

Thus the reader can see that the 115 acres we had bought presented every possible problem of farm management. No farm buildings, totally derelict boundary fencing, invasive sheep from every direction, wild Shetland ponies and the machair full of rabbits.

On the basis that one has to make a start somehow, I was lucky to invest in a wonderful milking cow, an Ayrshire cross Shorthorn which only cost me £39 10s. (£39.50) from a crofter in the neighbouring township of Northton who readily admitted that she was too delicate for him to cope with. The reason was her large teats, one might call them balloon teats, which when her udder was full of milk were very attractive to the clegs or horseflies which would bite the teats, causing big sores, and, of course, Kuchi would kick when you gripped the sore teats to milk her. However, I used to keep a tin of lanolin handy in the byre and apply this to the teats after every milking, which soothed them and helped to put off the flies. Additionally, when the flies were really bad in June I would keep her in the byre and would cut grass and take it to her, thus avoiding the flies completely. She yielded nearly 2,000 gallons of milk at every lactation, which I sold as liquid milk to our visitors, or I churned the cream into butter, again for the summer visitors staying at the Lodge.

Kuchi on machair grazing.

In that first year at the Lodge we decided to take paying guests for a modest weekly sum including all meals. My wife was such a kindly person that, when the assembled guests applauded the sirloin of beef which she had provided, they soon demolished it – their appetites in the sea air were huge – then she would yield to their request for a lobster. Anyway, after the first season of paying guests I warned Pat that we could not continue with that enterprise otherwise we would soon be bankrupt.

An American artist and his wife had a holiday with us but they chose to live in Laxdale Cottage seven miles from the Lodge – an old keeper's cottage – and left their two daughters to be paying guests with us. Unfortunately, the elder daughter Maro, about 13 years of age, tall and slim, had an appetite even bigger than a horse! In fact at normal mealtimes we found it impossible to satisfy her appetite. So after a month with us, she had almost eaten us out of any profit we were making from the other guests. Meanwhile her parents were relishing the month in the isolated cottage without the encumbrance of the two daughters. When they came to collect them, I suggested to the father that he might like to check Maro for worms, but he assured me this had already been done before leaving Italy, so I was bold enough to suggest that on returning to Italy they have a further check-up. A few weeks later he wrote me an apologetic letter saying that I was quite right in my suspicions and that the local hospital had removed with new medicines a tapeworm over a metre long!!

Because it is very difficult to make an adequate living from a normal croft, all men and women without family ties would look for seasonal employment – preferably on the island but more often on the mainland. The young girls, having just left school, were always much in demand by mainland hotels for seasonal summer employment as waitresses, chambermaids, etc. There was always a good demand for them because they were such reliable and well-mannered youngsters.

Thanks to the construction of a number of hydroelectric schemes the men, at this time, were very often able to obtain seasonal employment as labourers doing anything from drilling rocks ready for dynamiting, concrete mixing, shuttering-up concrete for dam walls – a whole variety of jobs for which they were well paid with lots of overtime and night work. Other men, particularly in Harris and Lewis, were recruited by the whaling firm Christian Salvesen which operated every year in South Georgia in the Antarctic, killing and processing whale meat in their factory ship. It is interesting that the medical officer supporting the whaling expedition, Dr MacIntosh, lived in Rodel, South Harris, and so Harris men felt very much at home in South Georgia under his care. The whaling men spoke highly of the doctor's skills but all were agreed that he was at his best, particularly for surgery work, when he was well oiled with whisky!

Returning to the sketch map of Borve Lodge and the farm, outside the farm boundary was Loch an Duin, a large freshwater loch from which Lord Leverhulme had piped water for the Lodge and its adjacent cottages. It had, on the rocky Duin, a colony of Arctic terns nesting there every year and because of its isolation the birds were pretty successful in rearing their youngsters. Against the roadside on the opposite side of the road from the Lodge, there was a yellow iris bog which adjoined the deep peat area, and the iris provided good cover for the occasional Corncrake and Water Rail.

Boggy peat area of the park after draining and reseeding.

Because of the state of the fencing, in many cases its non-existence, it was always in our early years a difficult problem deciding which patches of the farm to plough and plant with oats or potatoes or turnips. The amount of genuine good land for ploughing was very limited so it was a question of finding a suitable patch, a quarter acre or at most an acre of ground in which to plant the main crops.

Reseeded area in the park. MacLennan's croft on eastern boundary.

LIVESTOCK

Having sold the calves in the autumn, wintering the cows was always a worry, eking out the hay and oats and turnips to see a long winter through. My own philosophy was to feed the cattle quite well from January, into February and early March. Then, when they calved in late March or April, I would let the cows 'milk off their backs', using the accumulated fat of the good feeding they had had, to utilise the nutrients to feed the calf. In fact, I think it does most females of the animal species good to work off surplus weight feeding the young and to get them into condition for having the next youngster. So, waiting for the spring grass to start growing was always an agonising time, worrying about the condition of the cows and calves when they were battling to find something to eat, stocks of hay and oats having been finished.

As far as croft work is concerned, the average crofter will only keep one or two cows to provide milk for the house and one or two calves for the autumn sales each year. Hay for one or two cows to see them through the winter is easy to make, no matter how poor the summer weather may be.

For somebody starting real farming in an island situation you learn about the individual characteristics of the cattle under your care. For example, Trixie, my first calf, who in turn had several calves, could not be persuaded to eat a chopped turnip. Whether it was the smell I don't know, but she could be starving and still would not eat a turnip. So by studying the cattle as individuals, I could vary the ration of food according to their needs and their individual fancies. This study of the individual animal is especially important at calving time.

Kuchi was my first and best house cow. I was always with her when she calved; even if I sat up all night I would be with her and when she was calving she would turn her head and look at me as if saying, 'I am ready for a hand,' and as she strained I would just pull the forelegs of the calf to help her deliver the calf. When the calf was out, the cow would lick the calf dry and get it on its feet, and I would then take her into the byre to her standing. There was a window immediately by her head and I had put a board up to stop cattle pushing a horn through. From the outside this acted as a mirror and she would chew the cud looking at her own reflection in the mirror and you could see her watching herself chewing on the right-hand side and then making up her mind to chew on the left! This provided me, sitting on a three-legged stool milking her, with entertainment, seeing her enjoying her own reflection.

Kuchi calving was in stark contrast to the Highland cow Bridget. When she calved she would go berserk and actually toss the calf with her long horns and I had a difficult job calming her down. In fact, it is better for a Highland cow to calf outside in the field rather than in a box indoors, as it is more natural, and I used to put her out as quickly as I could, otherwise she would just bellow and toss the calf around. But there is no point with any livestock in losing one's temper and getting rough with them, as it just makes matters worse. Talking quietly will help to calm them down.

Another interesting individual characteristic is the cow that is the thinnest and most thoroughly woebegone in its looks will always move to the front of the herd when somebody is taking a photograph! Usually the worst-looking cows are the most generous in the amount of milk they give to their calves; they really milk off their backs and just give everything to their young. I still have my herd book in which I kept a detailed account of every animal I had with dates as to when they went to the bull and dates when they calved, plus any diseases or upsets that they had. So I owe a lot of my observational powers to the detailed observation of my individual animals.

A Welsh Black and cross highland cows with their suckler calves in the park.

In ten years I never lost a cow or a calf. All my cattle had an aluminium ear-tag fitted into the ear with special pliers. My herd number was IV173 and then the number of the animal. But in addition they were all invariably named after trees, e.g. Rowan, Willow, Beecher and Sitka. As a general rule it is not good to give names to lambs, because if an orphan lamb has been reared by the wife and the children of the family and they have become very fond of it, slaughter time causes a major upset when a 'member of the family' is sold.

My aims were to keep two cows for the milk requirements for our own family and our summer visitors. When surplus milk was available, I would separate out the cream and churn it for butter. In keeping with the development of improved pastures I created a steady increase in winter fodder production to build up a herd of 15 breeding cows which calved in early spring, their suckled calves being weaned and sold in the September sale.

Most of the breeding stock were bought as calves, preferably Beef Shorthorn x Highland, the latter providing hardiness to cope with the wet winters. In almost all cases the calves were malnourished, suffering from intestinal worms and mineral deficiencies. Happily at this time, ICI produced Minel, a mixture of minerals including cobalt with phenothiazine, an excellent cure for a range of worms and liver fluke. The Shorthorn blood in the cross breed provided an adequate supply of milk to rear a good suckled calf for the autumn sales. Having sold the annual crop of calves, the aim was to rotate the now dry but pregnant cows around the different grazings on the hill and machair until the winter compelled bringing them into the byres.

The same imponderables applied to stocking with only one or two corrugated-iron sheds for housing the livestock. This in itself was a limiting factor and so, in the early years, I limited myself to buying heifer calves at the local sales and rearing them as well as possible until they became heifers and then cows, by which time I hoped to have sufficient new accommodation to house them for the winter. This finally came together and these ambitions were achieved with a Hill Farming Improvement Scheme which I completed after six or seven years. A new byre was built out of the excellent huge garage which was attached to the Lodge and the big room over it was used as a hayloft, the adjacent outbuildings being invaluable as loose boxes for calving cows and young calves. By then, the herd had

Cross highlander with her Aberdeen Angus cross calf.

built up to 15 breeding cows, calving in March/April and suckling their calves through the summer until the autumn sales in September when the calves were abruptly weaned and sold at auction to mainland buyers. As a general rule, I cut sufficient grass to make one ton of hay for each cow which, together with about a quarter ton of oats fed in the complete sheaf, plus about five pounds of chopped turnips every day, formed a good ration to keep the cows during the winter.

It is of interest that, whether for the old byre or the new, I bought one-inch flooring timber from a demolition firm in Glasgow and this I put down as a form of decking on the concrete so the cattle lay comfortably on a wooden slatted floor with their dung and urine going through it and draining into the dung channel. This made mucking out every third day much easier and it was also much more comfortable for the cows.

Talking of housing, it takes a week or two for cows or heifers to become accustomed to their own particular standing so that when they are let into the cowshed at nightfall, they go straight to their proper standing where the food is stacked waiting for them – hay, oats and turnips. Given time, they automatically go to their proper places, but in the meantime patience is required to teach them where they are supposed to be. It does not pay to be in a hurry, otherwise you will end up with cows fighting one another for a particular position.

I always kept details of every animal so I always knew when a cow was due to calve and, as far as possible, I would see that she was moved from the cowshed into a loose box so that she was on her own and able to move round the box for calving.

The potential of calves that I bought at sales throughout the island could only be judged by their heads. If a calf had a good head on it, my reckoning was, get the diet right and remove worm infestation, then the calf would come right and turn into a good heifer. And this was indeed the case. Many a time at a local sale the crofters would think that the Sassenach was being a fool and buying rubbishy calves. Happily they were proved wrong and all the calves turned out very well. And in due course most of them produced a calf a year for six or seven years.

Wintering the sheep is another matter because they are simply turned out to live amongst the heather on the hill and providing they are not overstocked, namely about five acres of hill are allowed per sheep, they can survive the winter. It is only if there is serious prolonged snow that the crofters will start humping some hay up onto the hill to feed the sheep. But in the ten years under review, serious snow was never a major problem. Usually there would be quite a heavy snowfall at the beginning of January, followed by a week of glorious, still, sunny weather and from then on it was a case of rain and sleet rather than snow.

The Black-Faced sheep which I kept, about 50 in number, I kept with a fair measure of success, but after three or four years I decided to go out of sheep because the competition in the spring for the grass available was too great. So I decided to concentrate on the cattle and forget the sheep, and they were sold.

For any newcomers it is important to emphasise that, with lambs and calves, it is vital to dose them for worms at the first signs of seeing them standing still. When you see lambs and calves not thriving and not growing, not putting on weight, that is the time, don't put it off. Keeping livestock is a discipline; when a job is ready to be done, it must not be put off for another day, it must be done immediately. In fact, you could say that good husbandry requires strength of willpower to do it when it is absolutely right to do it and not later.

CROFTERS

Our nearest neighbours were Alec and Donald MacLennan who lived with their elderly mother and their sister Kirsty. Donald was not very strong but was able to help with the sheep on their croft. Alec was strong and a very skilled man with the sheep, particularly in regard to training and using sheep dogs. In fact, he was probably the best shepherd in our area. Old Mrs MacLennan, their mother, like many elderly folk on the island, was riddled with rheumatism, but contributed to the family income by knitting superb socks which sold very well and never wore out. They lived in a quite small corrugated-iron house, a bungalow, but subsequently built a stone house.

The next neighbour on the south side was Lachlan MacLellan. He was a very happy-go-lucky crofter with one daughter and a wife who had been in service before marrying. In some matters she was considered inexperienced and there were several stories illustrating this, such as when the fish van called, she bought a large conger eel, carried it into the house by the gills, went to hang it on the six-inch nail which was on the back door and as she hung it up, it turned its head and bit her. It was a live fish which still had some life in it as she discovered! We called Lachlan 'Lacky'; he was the sort of man who preferred to work for other people, rather than for himself. So he would very often be harvesting potatoes for a neighbour in October and it would be nearly Christmas Day before he would lift his own. Lacky did quite a lot of work for me at the Lodge and he never stopped telling stories, chuckling as he went. One of my favourites was the story of 'Mad Michael'. Michael was a crofter on North Uist. He was a fairly simple bloke with limited property. During the war he registered with the shipping pool in Glasgow ready to work on any ship that needed his services as an able seaman. He was lucky enough to get on a merchant ship which had a few passengers as well as goods. He was a big man and was permanently hungry, and as he passed the ship's galley he popped in and stole a string of sausages and tucked them inside his boiler suit and wandered out on the deck looking all innocent. The first mate saw him looking idle and said there was a stay on the mainmast which needed fixing and to climb up the mainmast and fix it. As he was climbing the rope ladder one of the sausages slipped out of his boiler suit. The passengers were getting quite excited looking up to see what the seaman was doing and the first mate shouted: 'Put it away, Michael, put it away.' Well, Michael was in such a position that it was not easy to put it away, so the easiest thing to do was to get the jackknife out of his belt and cut the sausage off and throw it into the sea – the passengers were horrified to see a black-backed gull swoop down and take it away as a titbit!

Lacky had a varied background; he had formerly worked for a Mr Beveridge who was the owner of a large lodge which still exists on the very northern tip of North Uist. Lacky was well versed in handling boats and fishing.

The next-door neighbour to Lacky was John MacDonald. John was a very good-natured crofter and had had a big family, all of whom had done well. One was headmaster of a big secondary school on the Scottish mainland and, as with many of the crofters' sons and daughters, he would come regularly to visit his parents during the summer holidays. John (and his largely untrained collie dog – nick-named ironically the 'Cup-Winner' by his neighbouring crofters) was getting on a bit in age for shepherding skills. I visited him one day to say hello to him and he pointed out his teeth, which were black stumps, and he said: 'Mr Wilkinson, can you help me because these teeth are rotten, they are black stumps, they are no use for cas-trating the lambs!' When John came to gathering the sheep, his fellow crofters always dreaded the moment when the communal drive brought a hundred or more sheep to the pens which were known as the 'fank'. When the sheep got near to the fank, John Mac-Donald – for sheer pride – would let loose the 'Cup-Winner' which, in spite of John yelling, would scatter the sheep right, left and centre. Finally he would take off his long jacket and hang it up by the sheep entry gate and use it to act as a blind to get the sheep turned into the gate. He would be waving and shouting in Gaelic 'haramasham' – usually it ended up with half a dozen sheep disappearing over the neighbouring hill with no hope of getting them back that day! John loved his sheep. Throughout the winter he would look after the hoggs, feeding them home-grown carrots he would painstakingly chop by hand.

I used to go through his croft with his permission to Sta Bay where over the centuries tides had produced graded gravel. I got my gravel for concrete block-making from there and sand from the next-door beach and fine gravel for pebble-dashing (harling). It was also a good bay for seaweed-gathering after a south-westerly gale,

so I would take the tractor and trailer and get several tons of bladderwrack and laminaria (tangle o' the isles).

*Alec at Sta bay gathering
sand and gravel mix for
block-making.*

*Alec carting laminaria
and bladderwrack
seaweed at Sta Bay.*

The next neighbour was Donald MacLeod, known to everybody as Dolly MacLeod. He had been a dispatch rider with the 51st Highland Division who took the lead in the Western Desert campaigns and in Italy during the Second World War. He was a very good shepherd. Occasionally his brother Lachlan would visit from Patagonia in Chile, where he was a full-time shepherd (a large number of shepherds in Patagonia were from the Isle of Harris; they were keenly sought after). Donald gained a useful income from craftwork, carving the rams' horn handles for shepherds' crooks. He and a mate went out to the island of Gaskir once a year in the autumn to slaughter a limited number of grey seal pups, from the skins of which he produced sporrans, purses and other craft articles for sale to tourists. He never killed more seals than were necessary for his own production and it seemed unreasonable to me that legislation put a stop to it. Anything that is appealing, say a seal or a badger, has an attraction which, I feel, leads to its total protection.

Next door – travelling south – was Finlay MacKenzie, a quiet man somewhat older than the rest of the crofters but a very capable shepherd and a good observer. Lord Leverhulme with his marketing of margarine had an advertisement in the popular press of a picture of woodland with pheasants hidden at all angles in the foliage of the trees. It was a competition where you had to count the number of pheasants you could find and then suggest a slogan for this new margarine. Finlay got the number of pheasants correct and his slogan, 'Pheasant brand margarine, worth its weight in butter', won the prize of £1,000. With the thousand pounds he built a very fine two-storey house for himself which is still standing. However, the house was abandoned by his only daughter Morag, who, marrying somewhat late in life, decided she needed a modern bungalow rather than renovate the old family house which was riddled with woodworm and which would require a fortune to restore. It was cheaper to build a new bungalow, subsidised by the government. Her husband was a fisherman and the bungalow is now surrounded by his lobster pots.

Finlay's next door neighbour was Alistair MacSween. A short man but very energetic, he always did well in the old age pensioners' race at the biennial agricultural show in Leverburgh. The first prize for the race was a full bottle of top-quality whisky which was attached to the tape, and it was amazing the speed that Alistair always produced to get that first prize. In addition to his energy, he had a very talented wife, Joanne, who was reckoned to be the expert at digging out sand eels which at low tide wriggle into the sand and hide. Joanne almost knew where they were lying. With a sickle she would hook them out from the sand – a tasty dish normally the chief food of the terns that nested on the island.

The last crofter in Scaristavore township, Angus MacDonald, was a very hard-working man. It is said that he used to get up at five o'clock on a summer's morning to sharpen his scythe by lamplight so that he lost no time in getting out to cut the hay crop. As a further demonstration of his energy, he was foreman of the little gang of local crofters employed by the council to patch up potholes in the road. He had had the opportunity of buying a second-hand lorry very cheaply, so it resulted in the council paying him both as foreman and also for his lorry carrying asphalt in small quantities to repair the roads. As an example of Scottish thrift Angus even got his fellow workers to push the lorry from pothole to pothole to avoid using fuel.

Next in line was the post office at Scarista. In the Highlands the position of postmaster/mistress is not permanent. However, once the applicant is successful they will have the post for life. In fact, when Mistress Morrison as she was known was successful in her application for the post office, it so upset another lady in the township who had failed in her attempt to get the post office job, she would walk an extra half mile to post her letters elsewhere. Once a bit of feuding goes on it can become quite intense, to the extent that one will cut off one's nose to spite one's face. Mistress Morrison was married to Neil Morrison and they had three daughters, Mary, Mona and Joina. Joina married a Lewis man who was lucky enough to be in the American Air Force with its considerable perks, so they lived in the States, post war. Mary took over from her late mother as postmistress and still holds the position although she is coming up towards the age of 90! And, for a time, she was my secretary when I was managing the Harris Crofters Association, manufacturing Harris Tweed, so there are no secrets between us; we worked very closely together. She also is renowned for her portrait in the trilogy written by Finlay J. MacDonald, one-time crofter in Harris, then author and BBC producer, who wove his stories around Scarista which was his home – and Mary MacDonald, as she is now known, was the Peggy in his books.

Neil was probably the most respected man on the west coast of Harris – a real gentleman always ready with advice and a kind word for anyone. As a result the post office became a sort of beehive to which any crofter needing to have a chat would gravitate to have a chinwag or a debate with old Neil. He was renowned for his debating ability, so much so that we all felt that he would have made a wonderful speaker for the House of Commons. His near neighbour, George MacDiarmid, would pop in there of an evening and deliberately get a debate going in an effort to defeat old Neil. This became such a habit that round about half past five or six o'clock other neighbours including myself would gather to witness the demolition of George by old Neil. George loved a debate and he would slowly but surely, and unaware of the doom that was impending, think that he was mastering old Neil and Neil would egg him on by giving in on various points until George was lulled into a false sense of security. When George was poised to deliver the *coup de grâce* Neil would suddenly produce a knife and stab him straight in the back! The assembled company would double up with laughter!

However, Neil knew when he met his match because Mrs Morrison knew how to handle him. When he suggested that I might walk up to his byre to view a new heifer that he had just bought she bridled and immediately said, 'You are not to take Mr Wilkinson up there to the byre, he is wearing good shoes and I have been telling you to clear the mud up, but you have done nothing – if he goes up there with you to the byre he will ruin his good shoes.'

In order to have peace, I said, 'Come on, Neil, don't worry about the mud, I will come on up to look at the heifer.' So we escaped from the kitchen and embarked on the climb to the byre. There was a smattering of mud and I said to Neil, 'Good heavens, Neil, what was your wife complaining about?'

He replied, 'She wasn't complaining, she was just exercising her tongue!', which was typical of Neil's philosophy.

The next day I had occasion to go up to the post office for the proper purpose of getting stamps and whatnot for letters. I went into the kitchen and Mrs Morrison was busy baking scones. I said, 'Where is Neil?' and she replied, 'He is up at the byre, he will be back soon.'

There was a strong east wind blowing which hit the back porch and door of the house. I heard this clatter of Neil coming in the door and kicking the mud off his boots before taking them off, then a draught came right through to the kitchen where the scones were being taken out of the oven by Mrs Morrison, who yelled: 'For good ness sake, man, shut the blessed door,' and typically he replied, 'I will, but let me get in first.'

After Neil had come in he said to me, 'You will be interested in the experiences I had when I was a keeper to Lord Townsend on his estate on the Isle of Skye, in fact if you would like to come with me I will show you one or two memories of that time.' So we went out to the lean-to tin shed which had access from the post office and Neil pointed to this landing net hanging on the wall.

I said, 'May I have a look at it?'

He said, 'Oh yees.' He spoke in a soft Scottish accent but it was through his teeth. So I picked up the varnished bamboo handle which just crumbled in my hand, leaving me with just the varnish off the pole; woodworm had reduced the bamboo to powder. Neil was only mildly concerned. 'That's the end of my landing net,' he said.

Neil was a mine of memories and information and he had a sort of mini-museum of ancient pieces from landing nets to, I later dis-covered, a muzzle-loading gun! When I saw this muzzle-loader I said, 'Is it still functioning?'

'Oh yees,' he said, 'it is still in good working order,' and to prove it he took it off the hooks by which it was suspended from the ceiling of the hut, put black powder down the spout of the barrel and then tamped it with a rod, poured in some heavy shot and just tamped that in position.

Then he said, 'I will show you now how it works,' and we went outside quietly. There were a couple of Hooded Crows perched on the roof of his poultry shed. He fired the muzzle-loader and one crow fell dead straightaway. It so terrorised the hens that were in the run that they went off lay for the next week. Mrs Morrison was 'not best pleased'. What a fine man Neil was!

The surgeon at that time in the Stornoway hospital, some fifty miles north on the Isle of Lewis, was Mr Norman Jamieson. He used to bring his wife and daughter down to Harris for their summer holiday every year for which they rented the one and only house on the island of Ensay. Old Neil would walk his house cow all the way from Scarista down to the port of Leverburgh, load it on a fishing boat and sail it across the two-mile Sound of Harris to Ensay, where it would be put into the water to swim ashore and graze around the house for the two weeks that the Jamiesons were on holiday to en-sure that their daughter had fresh milk every day! In fact, the two weeks on Ensay proved to be a wonderful holiday for Neil with just the cow to look after.

Earlier I mentioned that Neil was full of good advice and he took his position seriously as clerk to the township when the rota said it was his turn to be in charge for twelve months. The charge included keeping an eye on the Department of Agriculture bull. The bull was placed in the 2,000-acre common grazing so that all the crofters of that township of Scarista could take their one or two cows to be served by a pedigree bull, and at the end of the summer season the bull was returned to the mainland from whence it had come, for the Department of Agriculture to look after it for the winter. When Danny MacVicar passed by the post office, lugging a heifer at the end of a rope, taking it to the bull, Neil advised him, 'Now don't you be too long with the bull,' for should people leave their cattle with the bull too long, the bull would be too exhausted and would not be able to deal with the other cows brought to him. Anyway, it was the only time Neil was bettered by one of his fellow-crofters. Danny replied, 'Well, it will depend on the bull, not on me.'

This simple humour illustrates our uncomplicated way of life; we didn't need television which did not exist then. We created our own humour by telling each other stories which were true. We made our own entertainment visiting each other's houses – nobody ever knocked on a door. Providing the gale would allow it, you would walk in and shut the door quickly and were immediately offered a cup of tea because the kettle would be sitting on top of the stove ready and waiting. When a journalist who wrote a weekly article called 'The Scotsman's Log' for the *Scotsman* covering his travels in Scotland arrived in Harris, he said, 'One thing I did not discover and I am sure exists, but I think it is an island secret, is the location of the tea plantation in the Harris hills,' because he was offered tea everywhere he went.

Talking of newspapers, it is worth mentioning here that the one locally produced paper eagerly awaited and read by everyone in Harris was the *Stornoway Gazette*, printed and published on the Isle of Lewis. The editor was the renowned James Shaw Grant, an extremely capable, friendly and accurate journalist. The paper always published the results of competitions and particularly agricultural shows, giving a full list of winners of the cups, and sheepdog trials would get a full report. A worthy paper, it is still in regular weekly publication. The only other paper that could be purchased regularly

Balmain Capstan pedigree shorthorn bull on hire from Eishken Lodge, Isle of Lewis.

was the Scottish edition of the *Daily Express*. When its staff was on strike and we failed to get copies across the Minch from the mainland it is the one occasion in my life that I have written a letter to the press. I wrote to the *Stornoway Gazette* that the strike of the staff of the *Daily Express* in Glasgow was causing distress to me and others in the Isle of Harris because we were denied our daily firelighter! – I signed the letter 'crex, crex' (being the Latin name for the bird called the corncrake).

A relative of Neil Morrison was John Morrison who lived in the village at the foot of Toe Head called Northton. John had a simple garage just big enough to house his workbench and equipment, and one rather battered bus which served to carry passengers on regular visits to Stornoway 50 miles to the north. It also acted as the hearse for funerals so it carried many a coffin in its day, and served as the ambulance for the island. John would run severely ill patients up to Stornoway hospital for treatment. He was a portly man with a long-suffering wife Katie-Anne. Her real name was Kate but because there were a lot of Kates around she was known as Katie-Anne.

As I possessed a very ancient Ford Ferguson tractor, I had to call upon John Morrison with some regularity to come to sort out various mechanical problems on this original petrol/paraffin-fuelled machine. I would always entertain John to a dram of whisky and he would sit enjoying story-telling to me (and me to him) until he had

had several drams of whisky, and then about midnight he would say, 'We would best have a look at the tractor.' So I would take him away from the peat fire, he would put his cap on – he would never attend to any job without his cap, even if he was under cover – and in five minutes he would sort out the problem. He would never tell me what he had done, that was always a secret (after all, everybody has to make a living!). So he would have a final dram to celebrate the repair of the tractor and then go off home to head for bed with Katie-Anne, who had actually usually been long in bed before him.

He so much enjoyed coming to the Lodge to have a chat that one particularly foul night, with a Force 10 southerly gale blowing, I heard this car in the backyard come to a halt and the next thing I heard was the banging of the back door as John stumbled in against the teeth of the gale, putting his shoulder to the door to close it. He came through to the sitting-room where I had got a good peat fire and where I welcomed him with a whisky.

I said, 'Well, it's a foul night, John.'

He always said, 'Well, evallach it's a terrible night, but you have a good fire here.'

I said, 'And you have a dram in your hand.'

He replied, 'Slangevar.'

It was pitch-black outside and an awful gale was rocking the house, it was so bad.

I said: 'John, supper is ready, will you stay and have a bite?'

'Och,' he said, 'I had better not, I had best be getting home.'

And then I said, 'You had best have a stiffener for the road, we will have another dram,' and with semi-reluctance he accepted another dram.

Then Pat, my wife, put her head round the door and said, 'Darling, supper is ready, will you not bring John through for supper.'

But John said, 'I had best be going.'

I suggested, 'Use the telephone and tell Katie-Anne that you are having supper here and you will be back after.'

He persisted. 'I had best be going.'

But I said, 'It's such a foul night, John, why are you leaving?'

And he said, 'I had best be getting back,' and finally he said, 'I've left my wife in the car!' While he had been sitting with me, drinking whisky, she had been sitting outside in the car, in the back yard, in total darkness, in the teeth of the gale!

Now John Morrison loved his association with 'the gentry'. His great pal was Major-General Sir Colin MacVean Gubbins who had a holiday cottage in the village of Leverburgh, and John used to go out occasionally shooting with the general. He was also very friendly with Mr Lomas, who was the owner of Kyles Lodge, Leverburgh, and occasionally went out to sea in Mr Lomas's dinghy. John would come and have the occasional shoot with me, with varying success because he was not very clever with the gun. In fact, he reminded me of Mr Tracy Tupman of *The Pickwick Papers* who found that the ideal way of firing his gun for the safety of himself and all bystanders was to raise it vertically, close both his eyes, and squeeze the trigger!

John Morrison and Geoff, South Harris show.

John and I, at the end of the agricultural show held every other year in South Harris, would be joint auctioneers of the prize-winning cakes and handicrafts. We would sell them off in aid of the Show Society and because of his stuttering English he could not always find the right phrases to describe such a thing as the first-prize Victoria sponge. We would take it in turns to auction off individual items and John, having picked up Mrs MacKay's prize-winning Victoria sponge cake (Mrs MacKay was a wonderful, renowned baker who had so deservedly won first prize), stood on a desk, held the cake up for all to see and said, 'Och well, here is the prize-winning sponge baked by Mrs MacKay and what a wonderful opportunity, who will bid me for this prize-winning sponge, I can tell it's a winner by its weight!'

Mrs MacKay went ballistic – and if looks could have killed, John would have been dead on the spot!

Saint Columba came over from Ireland in the sixth century and founded the now famous abbey at Iona off the west coast of Mull. In the same period he established a Christian base at Rodel on the southern tip of the Isle of Harris where over the years the church of St Clement's was built.

As far as we know the second Irishman to settle in Harris was a handsome man, one Ted Cadden, who after wartime service in the Middle East was demobilised in London where he met and married Mary Morrison (sister of John Morrison, Northton). They decided to settle near her relations, buying a small cottage in Scarista which just had a walled garden of exactly one acre. Ted was very energetic and talented. He soon licked the garden into shape and enthusiastically grew a wonderful crop of main-crop potatoes. A neighbouring crofter had observed Ted carefully applying a white powder to the plants and he was bold enough to enquire of Ted the name of the powder. Ted replied confidentially that it was a light dressing of self-raising flour! (In fact, it was sulphate of ammonia, a readily available nitrogen manure.) The secret was soon out, with the result that the few grocery shops in Tarbert and Leverburgh were besieged by crofters stocking up on the magic flour!

Encouraged by the success of his potato crop which found a ready market Ted's enthusiasm got the better of him and he next planted the whole acre with cabbages, not a popular item of diet for a Harris man. Thus a good half of an excellent crop remained unsold. In spite of the odd setback Ted and Mary were very happy raising three lovely daughters and eventually they were successful in getting the tenancy of a croft on which he planted a dense tree crop, again demonstrating his skills as a not-for-profit plantsman. Incidentally Ted was always most hospitable and a great storyteller, but as far as I am aware he never revealed what he did in the war. All we knew was that he was a very fluent speaker of Arabic, leading to the surmise that he was perhaps serving in intelligence. Ted remained an enigma into old age.

Other near neighbours were Mr and Mrs George MacLeod. They had two sons, young George (George jnr.) and Big Angus who was much taller and stronger than most Harris men. Old George had been a keeper for Lord Leverhulme, and he lived at Laxdale Cottage, which was where he raised his family. The location of the cottage was strategic for keeping an eye on the River Laxdale, Loch Laxdale and Loch Fincastle for its salmon and sea trout. Now riddled with rheumatism he virtually spent his days hugging the 'modern mistress' which was the trade name given to a cast-iron cooking stove which was good for burning peat and coal. If it was not too hot George sat back in his easy chair with his feet up on the 'modern mistress', which suited his rheumatism. His wife, who was much the same age (they were both in their mid-eighties), was as active as he was idle. Behaving like a typical Sassenach when I visited one day, I said to her, 'There must be something that you eat, or take, that keeps you so fit and so active.'

'Och,' she said, 'there is nothing in particular.'

'Come on, Mrs MacLeod,' I said, 'there must be something which keeps you so bright and breezy.' But the more I questioned Mrs MacLeod the more she denied taking any special herb or medicine or anything.

However I persisted and eventually she gave way saying, 'Och well, I take as much Epsom salts as will cover a sixpence when I get up in the morning and I put them on the back of my tongue and then swallow a cup of tea.'

I said, 'Well, that is wonderful, would it not be a good idea to give George a dose of salts when he gets up in the morning.'

She said, 'Oh, he has it as well.'

Old George MacLeod let young George run the croft. He kept a few head of cattle, milking half a dozen cows for selling milk in the village. However, after one year of this George discovered that it was much easier to import milk from the mainland on the daily steamer coming over to Tarbert and to add on a profit margin and sell that rather than carry on battling with his small herd of milking cows and all the work involved.

Another local neighbour was Danny MacVicar who was away a lot of the year crewing on a Mediterranean yacht belonging to a rich owner. His wife Morag-Ann kept busy earning additional income by being the official stamper for the Harris Tweed Association. Genuine hand-woven Harris Tweed, the material itself, has to carry the official stamp of the Orb. Morag-Ann was paid by the Harris Tweed Association. Tweeds would be brought to her and the transfers ironed on. Morag-Ann had one child, Donald John, who in later years, beyond the purpose of this book, became a full-time livestock farmer on the Isle and was very good with livestock. Danny finally retired from his sea-going and settled back on the croft with Morag-Ann. But he was never as committed a crofter as the other township men. He fitted in well, but he was happier with an anchor and a rope rather than with a sheep and a cow.

John MacLeod deserves a special word; he had been living and working at Borve for many years as Colonel Walker's right-hand man. He was utterly reliable as a skilled chauffeur and above all a very fine ghillie, possessing great strength and an uncanny depth of knowledge on every aspect of the salmon which made the Laxdale river their spawning ground.

John was noted for his ability to control a dinghy (the Fincastle dinghy was of a near-perfect design known as a 'Kyle Boat', 13 feet long and 5 feet 6 inches wide; she was very stable and very responsive, especially with John at the oars) drifting it steadily down Loch Fincastle even in winds occasionally approaching Force 8.

Loch Fincastle was a loch with the river pouring out of it but with the dam wall made of quarried stone retaining peat behind it, of about one hundred yards in length and with sloping walls about nine feet wide and about twelve feet high. *(See Appendix VII for diagram.)* The peat had been finished with a good topping of cut turves which had settled over the years and been further consolidated by the numerous sheep that enjoyed the sweet grazing there. This structure had been very cleverly designed to cope with the highest spring tide levels because a westerly gale blowing in from the length of the estuary could see waves pounding against the wall. The dam was built by Lord Dunmore as a 21st birthday present for his son, Viscount Fincastle. (A number of other, although smaller so-called

'Dunmore Sandwiches' were built in the area to regulate water heights and flows, principally to enhance the fishing in various lochs and rivers.) There was an easy run up into the loch from the sea over natural rocky ground so that salmon and sea trout, with the spring tides of late June and July, could easily run up from the sea pool at the base of the dam wall into the fresh water of the loch. This, of course, required a spate because the normal flow of the Laxdale river was inadequate for fish to get up out of the sea into Loch Fincastle.

The loch itself was named after the son and heir. Like many sons and heirs, he was killed in the Great War so he never lived to enjoy the fishing there. Loch Fincastle was the favourite fishing loch and John MacLeod, the ghillie, knew every inch of its water and with his 13-foot dinghy he was able to hold the boat in half a gale, so that it drifted drifted slowly under his control the length of the loch whose axis was east–west.

The ideal weather for salmon fishing is a fresh wind blowing off the sea down the loch west–east, and that creates a nice choppy surface over which a wet fly can be repeatedly cast until a salmon is sufficiently irritated to seize the fly. Reference to the map will show the other fishings which provide sea trout and brown trout, but not salmon. Fortunately for me I had learnt to fly-fish for trout in the Pezi river which flowed down the Aberdare Mountains in Kenya but of course I had to learn what the favourite flies were for use in the Isle of Harris. The most reliable included Silver March Brown, Butcher, Black Pennel, Teal and Silver, Invicta and Peter Ross.

John's prolonged experience enabled him to know the favourite 'lies' of salmon and in these areas he would steady the boat and exhort the fisher to keep casting his wet fly in the hope of encouraging a fish

John MacLeod, our senior ghillie, with Edward Charlesworth and his first salmon.

to take. Always optimistic, John would suggest a change of fly such as switching from a rather sombre March Brown to a more brightly coloured Silver Butcher. Even if the morning had been miserable with continuous rain John would encourage his fisher by saying, 'You cannot judge the day until two o'clock,' when often conditions suddenly would become perfect for fishing. Perhaps another pattern of fly would be recommended which John could attach to the nylon cast with his horny fingers and thumbs, tying the knot as deftly as splicing heavy-gauge fence wire.

John never married, which is surprising as he was very fond of children and was always cheerful and patient with them. Perhaps he was altogether too comfortable at Borve living in the cottage by the entrance gate with Peggy, his unmarried sister, who proved to be a wonderful housekeeper. We were so lucky to have his help in his final run-up to retirement to his new croft house at Scaristavore.

It is fitting that this appreciation of vital characters should end with a special word for Alistair MacLennan who worked for us full time during our ten years at Borve. As a young lad he had worked for the Walkers at busy times of year. He lived with his parents in their croft only a quarter of a mile away. His one big disadvantage was due to him being an albino resulting in his extreme short-sightedness. This, however, did not prevent him from becoming a first-class builder and carpenter, indeed it enhanced his power of concentration. For example, when we were working together I would be distracted by a flock of high-flying geese passing over on migration, but as Alistair could not see them he would just press on with the task on hand.

Alistair was a wonderfully reliable timekeeper arriving to work on time whatever the weather. But I could never persuade him to work overtime! He quite rightly said that to do so would, in his case, reduce his effectiveness the following day.

He was gentle but firm in handling cattle and often took his turn hand-milking our two house cows. He loved our children and was always patient and helpful to them.

CROFTERS' CALENDAR

The areas under crofting are divided into townships and in looking at the crofters' calendar for the year's activities I will take the example of the township of Scaristavore consisting, as we have seen, of around ten crofters. Their hill land extends to about 2,000 acres going up to the peak of Bleaval. The sheep wander over the entire area in the little valleys and hidden areas as well as going to the far side of the mountain. Each year the crofters elect a clerk of the grazings and he has the responsibility of ensuring that the disciplines of crofting are observed. In particular, he sees to it that each crofter abides by his 'souming', which is the number of sheep and cattle that he may have on the hill. In addition, the clerk agrees with the crofters concerned when they will carry out their different gatherings of the sheep from the hill and starting with, say, 4 January, the sheep are all removed from the individual crofts and taken through the gates onto the common grazing and driven up the hill. The carrying capacity of the hill is roughly five acres for each sheep. This takes account of the poor quality of the grazing. The sheep are left up there all winter grazing on the grass and the heather until they are brought down around 11 April to be taken onto the individual crofts into their inbye land where they are confined on better grazing over the lambing period, which starts around 18 April.

Whilst lambing is going on, different areas of machair will be ploughed and planted with main-crop potatoes of the Arran Chief and Kerrs Pink varieties, the technique being to use a tractor with a two-furrow plough and at each turn of the tractor the seed potatoes are planted against the vertical furrow wall left by the tractor. The potatoes are planted every 15 inches against the furrow wall so that when the tractor comes round to plough another two furrows, the furrow slice is laid against the potatoes which are now six inches deep and 18 inches between the rows. Usually neighbours help with this planting, the men and women with buckets of seed potatoes, with each person doing a stretch of four or five yards putting the potatoes snugly in before the tractor comes again to bury them with the next set of ploughing. The seed potatoes have previously been prepared from the last year's crop which had been stored over winter in pits in the sandy soil of the machair. In the spring the turf is removed and the potatoes taken out and the smaller ones are all bagged up for seed and the bigger ones kept for cooking. The favourite manure for the potato crop is seaweed which has been carted during the winter gales from the shore and is spread on the grassland before ploughing.

Around 12 May, a further patch of land, either on the individual crofts or on a piece of common grazing, is ploughed for the planting of small oats. This is a variety known specifically as *Avena strigosa* which is harrowed in after ploughing, and a few days later a grass and clover mixture is sown on top of it and 'rubbed' in or lightly harrowed in. This grass grows with the 'nurse' crop of the oats so that after harvest the land is returned to pasture and hay. Quite a large number of crofters do not save their own oat seed but they could still order it from bigger crofters in North Uist and from one or two Inner Hebridean islands like Tiree.

One of the big advantages of the small or black oat, as opposed to the normal oat that is grown on the mainland, is that the whole sheaf of oats can be fed to the cattle during the winter. The small oats are digested by the cattle whereas with the large oats grown on the mainland the seed, if fed directly from the sheaf, cannot be digested and passes through with the dung of the cow. Another reason for growing the small oat is that it will tolerate the high calcium content of the machair land which is woefully short of manganese and cobalt. It is a crop, therefore, that is peculiar to the Western Isles. The final point with the small oats is although they are being planted in the middle of May they don't make much growth until late June and early July. Charlock (scallan) is the main weed, but its stiff stem helps to keep the oats standing in spite of heavy rain and gales.

About 15 May crofters commence cutting peat. Now is a good time to remind ourselves that the main rock formation on the Isle of Lewis, and for most of Harris, is 'Lewisian gneiss' which is totally impervious to water. This means that wherever there is a hollow area water gathers and sphagnum moss begins to grow. After about 50 years peat begins to form because the sphagnum moss as it grows and dies is simply preserved as solid vegetative matter, i.e. peat, and after one or two hundred years the deposit begins to become quite substantial.

Peat-cutting is usually done by two or three men with their wives assisting. A man cuts having first turfed the ground, the turves being thrown to one side. Then with a special peat-iron the man cuts slices of peat which are then caught by the woman and thrown up on the

Alistair MacLennan is standing in the uncut area with oat stooks opposite and Loch Cistavat in the background.

bank to dry; she is standing below the bank, the man is cutting and she is 'throwing out' as we say. Normally cuts are made two to three spits deep so one gets one slice of peat twelve inches long and then another slice below it and sometimes a third slice, all two inches thick, and these have to be thrown out, not on top of each other but carefully spread out. Therefore there is a skill to 'throwing out' the peats so the wind and sun can dry them. It is a time of year when both the old and the young are out peat-cutting; peat is the vital winter fuel supply and the doctor's surgery is always empty at peat-cutting time! An old man and an old woman may be on their last legs ready to die, but they will still go out and help with peat-cutting. The latest date to cut peat is 21 June if it is to be dry in time for winter fuel. In fact, that date, 21 June, is usually one of the later dates for lifting the peats, i.e. having got them half dry lying flat, you then put two slabs of peat upwards like a tower, then put one on top like building a model Stonehenge. This method enables the wind and the sun to blow right through the peats – it is known as 'lifting the peats'. From July onwards it is possible to stack the peats for subsequent carting.

I mentioned that the old do not attempt to back off from peat-cutting and stacking; both are social activities. But there are limits, and on the east coast of Harris the narrow road that runs its length is about 50–100 feet above the peat banks in the bog below. An old man in his seventies was carting the peat in his creel, which is a wicker basket tied to his back with a rope going round his chest, and he had been carting peat up this steep bank to the road all day. He was absolutely exhausted, but he stuck to the task until, nearing the top of the bank towards the end of the day, the rope broke and the creel fell off his back and all the peats tumbled down the hill. A passer-by heard him mutter, 'Oh Lord, what a relief!' Such is the patience and forbearance of the crofters.

By 23 June the barren ewes (those without lambs), and the tups are brought in to the communal fank for shearing, followed in mid July when all the ewes are brought in for shearing. The reason for the difference of time in the shearing is the fact that in a barren ewe and a tup the yolk in the wool rises several weeks earlier than in the ewes which are still milking and feeding their lambs. Left alone a sheep will shed its fleece naturally, allowing the new fleece to grow. By mid July the fleece of a ewe has 'risen' sufficiently to enable the shears to clip easily, removing the fleece in one piece. Usually one person will be busy rolling and folding each fleece which is then stowed in a large hessian bag ready for despatch to the Wool Marketing Board for grading and payment. When mid August comes

In the fank, sheep-shearing with hand clippers in July.

50

all the sheep are gathered with their lambs and they are all dipped in an acaricide dip to kill off ticks and keds. The dipping is done in a dipping bath in a section of the fank which is divided off for a swim-bath to be constructed. A pit is dug and lined with concrete; it is about six feet deep and about two foot wide at the top. The sheep are driven down a narrow race and are forced to jump into the bath and swim the length of the bath which is full of the acaricide solution. A man stands at one side with a short pole and dunks the head of each sheep as it swims along to make sure the entire body of the sheep gets the chemical on it. At the draining pens where the ewes and lambs stand for quite a while allowing the surplus dip to drip off them there is a shedding gate and as they are released, the ewes go through one side of the gate and the lambs through the other and the lambs are taken from the ewes and weaned. So it is dipping and weaning at the same time.

Of course, whilst this work is going on, the potato crop requires hoeing and then earthing up to make up a ridge over the growing plants.

On 12 September are the cattle sales when most crofters reckon to sell their calves at six months of age after being suckled by their mothers throughout the summer and weaned on the day of the sale. The auctioneers and buyers travel from Stornoway in a bus which contains the Bank of Scotland clerks and the Ministry of Agriculture official responsible for paying any subsidy for any calves being sold. They stop at given points around the island to where the cattle are dragged with rope halters and standing in the shelter of a stone wall a ring is formed of human beings and the auction takes place. In Harris the town of Tarbert had its own auction site, then they came on to Borve and thence to Leverburgh. A livestock lorry would follow the auctioneers and load up the cattle the dealers had bought and take them round the island to the ferry port of Tarbert ready for shipping to the mainland where the dealers sold them on in the big markets, particularly Dingwall. One of the biggest dealers, Mr MacRae, would buy up to a thousand head of cattle in the autumn sales and ship them to his home farm on the mainland. On one occasion he found that there was one beast short and such was his memory for livestock that when a year later that animal appeared in the ring in Stirling, he told the auctioneer, 'Stop the sale. That is my beast.' He proved it by quoting the ear-tag number which he had made a note of (e.g. IV173/4). He was a real gentleman. He told me he reckoned to make five per cent on all his purchases and since he dealt with several thousand head of cattle during the year, that provided him with a satisfactory level of income – large turnover of small margins.

By 18 September the oat harvest commenced. The oats were cut by scythe and tied into sheaves by hand using a band of stems of oats to wrap round the sheaf, knotted and tucked in. The oat harvest went on until mid October, often later, until the harvest was finished. Oats have to spend two or three weeks in the stook, drying thoroughly before they can be carted and stacked safely with no risk of heating.

Also in September the sheep sales took place on the same basis with the travelling team of buyers and auctioneers. So quite a lot of crofters sold their lambs and old ewes at the sheep sales, a very important time in the crofters' year. You could strip any crofter of any or all of his assets, except his wife and his sheep. The only time I have seen crofters going ballistic was when Spanish lobster fishermen came ashore and on the hill in North Harris shot two or three sheep to cut up and use as bait in their lobster pots. That really was as big a crime as murder in the eyes of a Harris man.

All sheep are given a keel mark with a wax stick which is usually blue or red behind the ears or on the middle of the back or on the hindquarters. Each crofter had his own keel mark. Most crofters knew their sheep as well as they knew their own children. If they were up on the hill and spotted a sheep with a blue mark on the hindquarters they would say, 'Ah yes, that is Alec MacLennan's sheep,' so that when they got back they could tell Alec MacLennan that one of his sheep was straying on the hill. The closeness of a crofter with his sheep is almost biblical. In fact it reminds me of the stained glass window in St Andrew's Church, Nottingham that impressed me as a child: a picture of Christ the Shepherd with the text underneath: 'Them also, I must bring'.

The crofters are busy lifting their potatoes by 16 October, usually done with a hand fork; it is helpful if several neighbours gang together to do the harvesting. It is a job easier done in a cheerful group of people rather than an individual struggling to do it alone. It is important to spread the potatoes in the sun and wind before bagging them up for carting to a pit, a pit being like a rectangular trench to take a coffin. The potatoes are buried in a series of pits, covering them with the turf. There they are secure for the winter, the frost being kept out by the turf cover, and because you dig the pit in the sandy machair soil, it does not stick to the potatoes. When they are taken out of the pit, they are nice and dry and ready for use as seed or ware.

Round about 13 November all the ewes are gathered in from the hill and dosed for liver fluke, ready for 21 November which is almost a sacred day in the crofting calendar. Almost all crofters put the tups in with the ewes that day and thereafter the crofter's wives are busy making a note when the individual ewes are served by the ram so that they know how the ram is performing. The gestation period for a ewe is 147 days. Early in January the ewes, now safely in lamb, are put out of the inbye land onto the hill grazings for the winter.

I have not mentioned that during October and November the autumnal gales bring their own harvest of seaweed to the shores which many crofters gather up and cart back to their crofts to allow to rot a bit before spreading it on the land for spring cropping.

An important point in the calendar round about 25 November is when the Scarista church holds a major communion service of the Church of Scotland. Contrary to the Anglican Church which has communion every week, the Church of Scotland only has communion at rare intervals. It is a very special occasion when friends come from Stornoway and all around Harris and Lewis to stay with their friends in Scarista for the communion weekend. It starts on a Friday and continues on Saturday and Sunday until they break up on the Monday. It is a time for friends to gather together and put their finest hats on which they buy by catalogue from a Manchester company which sends the hats in special hatboxes for approval or sale.

Many things are bought by post. When I complained that I needed to go 15 miles all the way into Tarbert to buy some bacon, Alastair MacLennan, who worked for me, said, 'Well, I could let you have some,' and I discovered then that he bought his bacon by post from Harrods in London. Through the grapevine he had got the news that Harrods sold their cheap cuts of bacon, mainly streaky bacon, with just a touch of lean meat in it while the rest was fat. Harrods sold this poorer quality bacon by post seven pounds weight at a time. I was glad to be put onto the same bargain and thereafter bought my bacon from Harrods. The crofters were not lacking in ingenuity so hats and bacon came by post!

It is worth mentioning that in the sixties the crofters' diet was simplicity itself. They would buy fresh herring at one shilling (five pence) for a score which they would then put in a wooden barrel, adding a thin layer of salt and then more herring and another layer of salt until the barrel was full. Their winter food was invariably boiled herring with Arran Chief potatoes which were much favoured because they were dry and floury and they absorbed the fat and the salt out of the fish, making it more palatable. Cakes and puddings were really unheard of and vegetables limited to the odd turnip or cabbage. Many crofters in the Western Isles suffered from blood pressure, which I think was induced by the high salt content of their diet together with the very acid drinking water (pH 3.6).

Geoff with Major-General Sir Colin MacVean Gubbins, visiting for the winter shoot of woodcock.

SOUTH HARRIS AGRICULTURAL SHOW SOCIETY

About this time, the early 60s, Dick (Mrs Walker) gladly made available the big loft above the garage for adult education classes during the winter. John MacLeod, of The Glen, Leverburgh, was the organiser and tutor for evening classes in carpentry. The big loft was equipped with basic benches, and about a dozen local men each had a carpentry project to work on – one evening per week – and hopefully were able to complete it during the long winter months. John MacLeod was a highly energetic and effective teacher. Pat and I decided to do a two-piece bookcase. Pat did her piece in one winter, but my piece took two winters because I was so busy chatting to fellow students!

John MacLeod, who was based in Leverburgh, suggested that it was about time South Harris considered forming a show society in order to mount a show in alternate years. He felt sure we could put on a very exciting display of livestock and vegetables and handicrafts – far better than North Harris, based in Tarbert, was doing once every two years. So, fairly speedily, I found myself 'lumbered' as the chairperson of the South Harris Agricultural Society and it was decided to put our first show on in August 1968. We were lucky to have an enthusiastic president in the form of Major-General Sir Colin Gubbins, KCMG, DSO, MC. Having retired from the army, he had a cottage in Leverburgh and was very keen to be helpful as Founding President. So a meeting was held in the Leverhulme Hall in Leverburgh and office-bearers appointed. It was agreed that membership would be offered in the society for a very modest subscription which, importantly, would entitle the member to exhibit in the show without any further payments. This was a great encouragement to the crofters who had very limited disposable income.

All the crofters in charge of the different sections of the show were great characters. My vice-chairman, Duncan MacLennan of Quidnish, was not only a great character but was also the image of the Hollywood actor Spencer Tracy. He was a county councillor, so had a wide area of friends upon whom he could rely.

Our show was held on the sports field of the secondary school in

Leverburgh, of which Mr MacIver was the very upright and serious head teacher. We had the official use of most of the classrooms for the displays of Harris Tweeds, knitted socks and also a section for our catering classes with their assembly of delicious sponge cakes, scones, etc.

The handicraft section, for which there was fierce competition amongst the exhibitors, included Harris Tweed dominated by Marion Campbell of Plockrapool. Marion Campbell was renowned internationally for her hand-woven tweed. She was not married, so devoted her efforts for the benefit of her two nephews, for whom she demanded replica cups for the numerous occasions when she cleared the decks of all opposition. It is pleasing to mention that Marion Campbell was so well known that she was awarded the BEM for her good work promoting Harris Tweed.

John MacLeod, the instigator of all this, was the show society secretary and, once the pressures were on as we approached the show day in August, he found it necessary to augment his normal energies with a touch of the 'old stuff'. Mr MacIver, who was a very religious man, did not approve, so I was a bit surprised as the whisky was flowing on show day, when John MacLeod said to me, 'Come and have a dram,' and he led me off towards the head teacher's house. However, it transpired that, knowing Mr MacIver's susceptibilities, John had diplomatically chosen the head teacher's peat shed in which to secrete his bottle of whisky, so we hid in the peat shed and had our drams – glasses were provided! Poor John – sometimes by the end of the show he found difficulty attending to his final duty which was to read out the prize-winners and call them up for collecting their prizes. Occasionally his diction got a little garbled what with all the MacKays, MacClennans and MacLeods; there was ample scope for confusion, to the distress of the guest of honour who was presenting the prizes, but John MacLeod himself was oblivious, too much in a haze of the 'real stuff' to worry.

We used the playing field for all our events, which ranged from the parade of cattle to the sports events of throwing the hammer and tossing the discus which left their mark upon the field because, to create this playing field, large quantities of willow branches had been put down on top of the peat bog before further soil was added and then the turf, so when the cattle were charging round the ring the whole ground shook and quaked and the hooves dug deep into the soft turf. We were worried when it came to putting the shot that the heavy ball used for the purpose might disappear through the crust into the bog beneath.

The old-age pensioners' race, which was always most popularly subscribed, was usually won by a diminutive 80-year-old, Alistair MacSween, who ran as light as feather across the 'bog' to grab the first prize which was always a bottle of whisky at the tape at the end of the run. The pounding of more portly OAPs was quite a thrill for the crowds surrounding the ring, cheering them on!

Geoff opening the South Harris Agricultural Show, Leverburgh, 1982.

I took my role seriously as founder chairman of the society and in my spare time would tour the island recruiting new members and when the chairman actually visited an outlying croft in all weathers, the poor crofter really could not refuse the very modest sum requested for membership. I owe it to this activity that I knew practically all the crofting families on the island.

Further examples of the benefit of membership would be to organise one or two agricultural outings each year, hiring the one and only bus belonging to the great John Morrison of Northton. We would, for example, go up to the neighbouring Isle of Lewis to have a look at some agricultural improvement project that they were proud of. Such outings were technically valuable and socially most desirable and usually accompanied by more than one or two drams, especially on the return journey. The heaviest drinker was Donald

MacLennan, a great friend of mine who, when he was in his 'cups', would stagger the length of the bus and come and sit on my knee and make sweet murmurings in Gaelic to my utter embarrassment.

However, usually the whisky got the better of him and he would have to make a hasty retreat to the folding door of the bus, to hang his head out in order to relieve himself of some of the alcoholic burden. As we went up hills and down again on the 50-mile trip we had to keep yelling at him to keep his head in as the folding door would keep opening and closing and there was the danger of him getting guillotined as he was offloading some of the whisky: 'Donald, get your head in!' We were always greatly relieved to pull up at his croft and discharge him into the arms of his plump and very happy wife Effie, who knew how to get him to the front door and sit him down and get a cup of tea down him and, with a large family, he soon sobered up.

Donald was the live wire of the village where he lived and he was self-appointed advisor to his neighbours, and others further afield, on the delicate subject of how to deal with the welfare officer when he was inspecting a croft house to determine what level of National Assistance should be given to the widow occupant or the elderly crofter. Given prior notice, Donald would make an appointment to visit as it was a serious matter. He would tell the crofter, 'Now, is that coal you have in the bucket there?'

'It is,' said the crofter.

'Well, get it away out of sight, into the shed,' said Donald.

So the bucket of coal would immediately be removed and dumped in the shed or the byre. And then Donald said, 'I see you have a stair carpet. You have got to get that up now.' So out came the tack remover and the rather threadbare carpet was lifted immediately and stowed away in the shed. By the time all the advice had been carried out, the house was pretty nearly stripped of any comfort that it might have had in time for the visit of the welfare officer. Gaelic-speaking people loved getting their vowels in a mess so the welfare officer became the 'Farewell Officer' so when the 'Farewell Officer' came to inspect, he nearly burst into tears as he tried to tick the boxes in his questionnaire; about the only box that he could tick was that the owner was present! Coal: nil. Peat: nil. Stair carpet: nil …

It was worth a bottle of whisky for any crofter to get advice from Donald because it was guaranteed he would get maximum social security benefits!

Whilst Donald was thus gainfully employed, Effi of the ample kindness, who was a most placid character, a lovely mother and a perfect wife for Donald, could not neglect her duties. This included milking the house cow, and occasionally I would go through to the byre at milking time and chat to her as she was milking. She was able to perch on an upturned bucket rather than have the luxury of a milking stool, and she clutched in her left hand a rather rusty wartime dried-milk tin into which she milked with her right hand.

In fairness to Donald he used to leave his family to look after themselves and go off to the mainland to work on hydroelectric schemes as a skilled labourer, to earn sufficient money to see them through the winter when he would return home. Harris was known as a reservoir of willing workers and they networked with a relative or friend who was a foreman of a gang working for contractors on building hydroelectric dams, so they could be guaranteed a place if they crossed the Minch to get work.

Of course, a witness to excursions was the redoubtable one and only John Morrison of Northton, who would be only too pleased to drive the bus to take us on outings. I saw so much of John that we struck up a rather unusual friendship, inasmuch as I would invite him to come to the Lodge on his way back or going to Stornoway, but preferably on his way back, and he would come in and have a dram or two with me before carrying on the remaining seven or eight miles to Northton where his home and garage was. He quite enjoyed my selection of records and so, having got him settled with a glass of whisky in his hand by a good fire, I would say to John, 'Now I am putting on a good record for us to enjoy.' My favourite at that time was a Peter Sellers LP entitled *Songs for Swinging Sellers* and we would sit back and listen to Peter lampooning 'the good old days' in his Lord Badminton's memoirs.

With so many friends on the island, 'first footing' at New Year was always a challenge and I would leave home on foot and walk the length of the township after midnight, calling in to take a dram with the individual households between the end of the village and the Lodge. Never less than three fingers of neat whisky was poured for the visiting Sassenach and he was too good-mannered to refuse it and then to the toast 'slangevar' the dram had to be downed in one swallow. I was glad that I no longer had my tonsils, so it was only the gullet that felt on fire! To be fair, the dram was usually followed by a little metal tray which bore a piece of fruitcake, a scone covered in crowdie (home-made soft cheese) and blissfully a cup of tea – and then one moved on to the next house for similar treatment. By the time I got back to the Lodge my legs were having a problem getting me into the kitchen where I shed my shoes, got hold of the anthracite hod, removed the plug from the Aga, stood back to avoid the minor explosion of gases and then poured in the whole hod full of anthracite. This was a nightly procedure but on this occasion had to be done carefully because of my delicate condition. Having done that final duty for the day or night, I would creep upstairs in my stockinged feet and quietly get alongside the double bed. Even a mouse would have been envious of the stealth involved. But then the peace was shattered by my wife shouting at me, 'Don't come near me, don't come near me!' She could smell the whisky before I got into the room!

VEHICLES

From a transport point of view, John MacKay was a key man with a readily available lorry for general transport work. Like his opposite number, John Morrison of Northton was an equally affable character. In these early days he was a one-man band, collecting and delivering coal from Tarbert, which had been shipped over from Greenock. He imported hay and straw from the mainland, and feeding stuffs – he was always in demand. But when we had the agricultural show at Leverburgh he volunteered his lorry to help take livestock to the show without charge. His wife Mimi was a perfect wife, bringing up a family of three daughters and two sons, all of whom have been a success. She ran a small shop attached to their petrol pump selling odds and ends of groceries, and she was always kindness itself, very welcoming to campers who would camp on the sand dunes close by overlooking Horgabost Bay, supplying them with water and essentials.

In the 1960s a steadily increasing number of crofters were investing in a second-hand car or van. Because of their vintage the speed of travel was almost self-regulating. I remember there was one exception: this was a high-powered, but ancient, Standard Vanguard saloon which belonged to a young mason, Donald MacKinnon, who lived in Leverburgh. He was the leader of a gang of four mates who were lucky enough to be employed on a sizeable project in Tarbert, building a large boarding hostel for students attending the inter-island secondary school there.

For the daily round trip of about 50 miles the Vanguard was the ideal vehicle – spacious, very comfortable and, when required, powerful. After a hard day's work on the building site the lads were anxious to get home, so when they came to the one really good straight stretch of road running past the manse at Scaristavore, they yelled at Donald 'to put his foot down' and 'go for it'. However, on this occasion one of the back-seat passengers was alarmed by an unusual rattling noise which he reported to Donald, who, concentrating on the narrow road, simply yelled to him 'to shut his bloody door p… p…properly'. When told that the door was firmly shut he realised that something was seriously wrong with the engine, whereupon he stuttered, 'B…b…bugger me, it's a b…b…big end.' The only question now for a 'banger', will it be a hen-house or peat shed? One never was quite certain whether cars dumped near a croft house were still sound in wind and limb or merely housing for dry peat or a shelter for poultry!

The MacDonald brothers, who lived at Luskentyre, were keen restorers of clapped-out vans, but I was not aware of their habits. At three o'clock one morning I was heading home from the east side of the island, with my lights deliberately off (there is always enough light in a summer sky to see your way). I spotted this van a quarter of a mile ahead of me heading towards Loch Fincastle and I thought, 'Ho, ho, these are poachers on the way to do their foul deeds,' so I quietly followed at a discreet distance and followed the van through to Luskentyre where I abandoned the chase, turning the car round and going limping home. The next day I had a word with someone who knew the MacDonald brothers well and he said, 'Don't worry, they are repairing the odd van and then they take it out for a test drive at three o'clock in the morning, knowing that the one and only policeman, who is based in Tarbert, will be fast asleep, so they are quite safe to drive at that time – without a licence!'

Another van that caused me some anguish had the registration number – still indelibly etched upon my mind - RCS 147, and I never did discover who that belonged to. I fancied the couple in it were courting and I did not wish to disturb them. Their favourite parking ground was in a quarry – giving them some additional privacy. It is interesting that my third daughter, who has a good memory, still can reply – after 50 years – when I ask her what the number of the van was: 'RCS 147', whereupon I give her the usual congratulations on her memory.

In those fairly early days of vehicle ownership, money to buy a really good second-hand car just did not exist. Most crofters were happy to buy a vehicle that had just passed its MOT and at the end of a year it would finally die-the-death and then be dumped in a quarry or, worse still, alongside the crofter's house to rust away – so the county council were periodically driven to go round the island gathering up the wrecks and shipping them away for scrap. Rust was a timely reminder that, by living by the sea with the salt-laden winter gales, the bodywork of the average saloon car would soon resemble a rust bucket.

DOCTORS AND DENTISTRY

For quite a long time Dr Wood, with his house and surgery in Tarbert, was the main doctor for the island. His father-in-law had been the general practitioner before him. When Dr Wood arrived in Tarbert to assist the elderly doctor, he fell in love with the doctor's daughter, Babs, and they in their turn had three delightful daughters: Augusta, Dorothy and Christine. The girls formed an enchanting trio, and to listen to them singing Scottish songs and country airs with a guitar accompaniment was an agreeable way to spend an evening.

Dr Wood was a very kindly person, as was his wife, and he was followed at a later date by another equally good doctor who had his own methodology of handling patients. This methodology was that the patient who had arranged the appointment had to strip off and stand naked for inspection no matter whether the trouble was an ingrowing toenail or a wisdom tooth or a boil under the armpit! The elderly ladies found this a great deterrent, so they had to think seriously before entering the doctor's surgery in the knowledge that they would have to totally strip off as a preliminary.

Attached to his surgery was a small additional area reserved for a dentist who travelled the islands 'butchering' as he went because usually the crofters' teeth were in such a bad condition they would have to be in agony before they went to see the dentist, and the only hope then was to have the wretched tooth extracted as it would be beyond repair. Horror stories of the dentist travelled round the island like a grass fire.

When the road surveyor took his young son in for some heavy drilling treatment and they arrived at the surgery, young Tommy took off and climbed the nearest tree in the garden and yelled that the last thing he wanted to do was to give up the safety of the tree and go into the dentist's chair! In the end, Dr Wood and the dentist combined to call in the local fire engine from Tarbert and a strong ladder was put up against the tree and the wretched boy was hauled out of it. There was no escape for Tommy.

One of the joys of being a doctor on the island was that owners of salmon fishing were only too pleased to let the doctor have a free day on one of their best lochs, so Dr Wood fished Fincastle on several occasions with good results. I would like to have seen more of the doctor and his wife socially, but they were highly committed scrabble enthusiasts – which is the one game I cannot enjoy.

SHOPPING

The shops in Tarbert and Leverburgh were often akin to minor department stores. Their shelves were piled with socks and tweeds and miscellaneous boots and shoes and, encouraged by the competition of others, they would even stock a reel of barbed wire or some loose butter – you could get more or less anything at these shops. As chairman of the South Harris Agricultural Society I helped a number of them in drafting their advertisement for the agricultural show catalogue. I remember Kenny MacSween of Strond, who had a small grocery store, included in his advertisement: 'everything from nylons to barbed wire'!

A little shop in Tarbert near the pier head was owned by Mary Flora MacCaskill and she sold bread and cakes, both baked in Stornoway and delivered daily to her shop. She was one of my chief buyers of a bag or two of early potatoes – I looked after them well on our farm, growing chitted seed so I always had the first potatoes ready for sale in the early summer at the end of June. I could never supply Mary Flora with enough of the early potatoes because, in commercial terms, they were what we called 'bag-openers'. Tarbert housewives would flock to the shop to buy early potatoes but at the same time be unable to resist the temptation of a cream sponge or chocolate cake fresh down from Stornoway.

HARRIS CROFTERS
ASSOCIATION

The farm at Borve Mor, which has been mentioned earlier when a Dr Robertson owned it as a 'hobby farm', eventually became part of the estate of Borve Lodge. The old farmhouse and its associated barns formed the headquarters of the Harris Crofters Association. It sounds a grand set-up but, in truth, was far from it. The ground floor provided an office for me and Mary Morrison, our general secretary. Another room provided a safe room for all the different Harris Tweed patterns and specimen twists of wool of all the different shades that went into the production of tweed. This 'holy of holies' was presided over by Donald MacLennan who was a prime example of a man with extraordinary talents which enabled him to identify every colour and which mill in Stornoway had produced it. For example he could look at a bit of grey yarn and say: 'This is S.A. Newall's Grey/5.' Another grey yarn: 'This is MacKenzie's Grey No. 20.' And yet a third grey: 'This is Smith's Grey 6,' a gift of colour differentiation which is usually the province of ladies and only rarely found in men.

The pattern room was important to us because we produced a number of pattern books in which nine by four-inch squares of material were clipped together forming a pattern book, which we sent to our agents in several overseas countries, notably Australia, South Africa and New Zealand, where Harris Tweed was much sought after for the winter season. The top pattern in the book was always very colourful and was a 'bag-opener'. It was designed to attract the eye of the beholder. The 'bread and butter' orders for useful quantities of tweed were for the old grey herring-bone patterns plus some browns for locals.

Our agents in the overseas countries were given a useful commission on sales. Amongst our agents was Mr MacDonough, who lived in Melbourne – he was the prize-winner who could never get enough tweed from us. I had travelled to Melbourne several times but I had never seen the expected amount of people wearing heavy tweed. Mr MacDonough was so impressed with our quality and output that he put Mary, Donald and me into a panic when he said that he must come over to the UK to see 'our operation'. The trouble was that he meant it! And the day dawned when I had to go up to

Stornoway to meet him at the airport. So I then had to rally our other troops, consisting of Lacky and George MacDiarmid who were busy in one of the barns warping yarn and bagging up cops of other yarn for the weft, ready for dispatching in our van to crofter weavers – especially up in Lewis.

The Harris weavers you could call fair-weather weavers. They were active during the war and immediately after, when they could sell tweed in any quantity such was the thirst for it on the mainland after years of clothes' rationing. However, when there was a return in peacetime to a more orderly market, the Harris weavers backed off and we had to find most of our weavers in the Isle of Lewis. This meant that once a week George MacDiarmid was doing a high mileage visiting crofts all the way up to the Butt of Lewis, picking up the finished tweeds and leaving them with the warp and weft for the weavers to get another piece of tweed made ready for picking up the following week. He took the finished hand-woven tweed into Stornoway to the finishers, Kemp & Co., who washed it, dressed it and packed it up for export overseas.

It doesn't require a brilliant mind to realise that this was an un-sustainable business in the long run. The failure of one American company to pay for one big order was a sufficient setback to cause us to make a decision to close the operation down, so, having been manager for a couple of years, I was then appointed liquidator for a year for the 'final curtain'. With all our shareholders being Harris crofters, I was determined that they and the mills from whom we had been buying all our yarn should be paid out in full, as we had outstanding debts with them. All this led to salvaging whatever we could to pay our debts.

Happily, at that particular time there was a high demand from the weavers for yarn from the mills in Stornoway, from whom we obtained most of our yarn. The yarn for the weft was on cardboard cops, and any surplus (because we were never exact in our purchase of yarn for a particular order) was stored in sacks in the barn. The sacks were a bit reminiscent of the typical Scotsman's sporran – when he opened it to get some cash out the moths flew out first! All these bags with surplus yarn were riddled with moths, but we picked them over and threw out the worst yarn and the rest were the best cops showing on top of the bag. We took them back to the mills, who were only too pleased to take them back and credit us. It was all done at Stornoway so quickly and they passed the cops on to hungry weavers who were desperate for yarn. Therefore I managed to pay off pound-for-pound all the Stornoway mills and then, by selling the Ferguson tractor and trailer to a buyer in Stornoway, plus other farm implements, I managed to pay off our crofter shareholders pound-for-pound. Altogether a very successful liquidation. Mercifully, all this happened after the official visit of Mr MacDonough. Needless to say he sent us a message of condolence when we closed down our operation.

Of course the tractor and trailer had to be delivered to Stornoway, 50 miles to the north, the tractor having no cab and it was just an open trailer. Lachlan MacLellan (Lacky) and I took turns in driving the tractor, winding our way up to Stornoway, cresting the hills of North Harris in January sleet and snow! After about ten miles at the wheel, we would do as best we could to snuggle down in the empty trailer, wrapped in a blanket to see if we could thaw out ready for another ten-mile driving stint later on. I think it is the coldest I have ever been – every part of me that could go numb did go numb.

NEIGHBOURS

In our first year or two at Borve, Mr and Mrs Lomas, who lived in a neighbouring lodge, were always very keen to entertain us and other folk visiting the island. They had a small estate in South Harris, based on their home of Kyles Lodge which had been built on the northern shore overlooking the Sound of Harris. They had some salmon and sea trout fishing, which they shared with the Rodel Hotel, based on the river that ran from Loch Langavat down through Loch Na Moracha to Loch Steisavat with the river finally running out into the mill pool in the centre of Leverburgh. Kyles Lodge had the fishing for three days a week and the balance was fished by Rodel Hotel visitors.

When Lord Leverhulme died in the early 1920s, his landholdings in Harris were quickly put to auction. One of these was the lodge at Luskentyre and another was the mini-estate of Kyles Lodge. The buyer of these two holdings was a Londoner, the owner of the Bell Foundry of Whitechapel Road who, as a speculator, had attended the auction in Harris when Lord Leverhulme's estate was divided up. His daughter Margaret fell in love with Lord Leverhulme's resident engineer, Mr Lomas, and they married and settled in the Kyles Lodge property. Mr Lomas kept himself occupied primarily in his 'snug hut' in which he had installed his amateur radio equipment. He would spend an hour or two regularly every day calling up friendly wireless 'hams' all over the world. He also enjoyed entertaining anybody who was visiting and at a loose end, because he had a dinghy with an outboard motor and enjoyed taking them out sea-fishing or simply sailing in the Sound of Harris.

They came to rely upon Pat and me having Saturday night supper with them. Mrs Lomas was a large and generous hostess; she always wore her own hand-knitted garments with heavy, broad stripes running horizontally which exaggerated her size. A dress-designer would say that, for the bigger woman, vertical stripes would be more flattering than horizontal stripes, but she ignored such niceties. She always had a weekend order with her butcher in Leverburgh, and likewise groceries and bread supplies were never reduced – they were kept at a high level. So the cool larder was always heavily stocked with uneaten loaves of bread and half-finished joints of beef and so on. Much of the surplus food was put into the backyard for the benefit of a flock of starlings that wintered at the lodge. The local sheep were quick to identify this new source of food and would gather round in the backyard, rams included, waiting for the daily spread of perfectly good loaves of bread. One morning when Mrs Lomas had a very bad cold she was late getting up and the sheep, led by two mature rams with their curly horns, got so restless that the rams charged the back door of the house so hard that they took it off its hinges and then invaded the larder and attacked the loaves of bread on the larder slab. When poor Mrs Lomas finally got down into the kitchen she was shattered to find a blast of air with the back door off; also the door to the larder was broken and the two rams were on their hind legs eating the bread off the shelf – they were not prepared to delay their breakfast any longer!

One particularly wild Saturday night, with a gale blowing and heavy snowfall, Mrs Lomas said very kindly to Pat and me, 'You must stay the night; it is too rough for you to drive back to Borve with the road now covered with an inch of snow.' The house was full of ornaments and memorabilia of one sort or another and the three young cats were allowed to sleep indoors, particularly in rough weather. Pat and I went up to the guest bedroom with some trepidation, passing en route a fine stag's head mounted on the passageway wall adjacent to a grandfather clock. During the night we were awoken by cats howling and cursing one another and then we heard a tinkle of bells as they took off from the grandfather clock. The three of them landed on the stag's head with such force that the nail holding the head gave way causing the head to thump down the stairs, taking the cats with it! This, in turn, disturbed an *objet d'art* which had fascinated us for many a month; this was a vase on the chest of drawers in the passageway to the bedrooms. In the neck of the vase a guillemot egg had been placed, and because it had been there so many years, the egg had sunk gradually into the narrow neck of the vase. Any attempt to remove it was impossible and it had become part of the vase. Nevertheless, it was an ancient entire egg (nobody had blown it to remove the yolk), so it had slowly generated more and more hydrogen sulphide until the cats from the stag's head hit the vase as they fell, causing the egg finally to explode from pent-up gases, all over the stair carpet. The two dogs, one ancient dachshund plus one springer spaniel, had come up the stairs and done their best to lick the carpet clean. The springer spaniel was so ancient he had a look like leprosy all round his nose which, at the age of fifteen, didn't improve his looks. Having done the cleaning-up job, as they saw it, the dogs retreated to the sitting-room downstairs where they each had their own chamber pot with regularly changed drinking water. Our one night there was enough!

One of the regular visitors to Kyles Lodge was Professor Heslop-Harrison, a professor at Durham University. He used to come up every summer for at least six weeks' botanising, particularly on the offshore islands in the Sound of Harris where he was taken by Mr Lomas in his dinghy with the outboard motor. Having had a good spell enjoying Mrs Lomas's hospitality, the professor then moved to Borve Lodge before we settled there and enjoyed similar hospitality from Dick and Colonel Walker. He enjoyed service from the maids, good food and drink, and trips out in the sea boat, so he had a very nice long vacation from the university.

One memorable Saturday night, with six inches of snow lying, Pat and I drove in our Land Rover the seven miles from Borve to Kyles Lodge for an evening with the Lomases, and a fellow guest arriving at the same time at the front door was Lady Gubbins, who had come from her cottage nearby in Leverburgh. Both she and Pat took their suede boots off and left them in the porch and put on a pair of court shoes for the evening's entertainment. We had a very good meal and the snow continued to fall. We decided we would not want to be too late setting off home so we went into the porch and the ladies put their boots on ready to walk in the snow to get to the cars. We heard a peculiar sort of squelching noise as we walked after we had said goodbye and Mrs Lomas had shut the door, so we were out of earshot. It speaks volumes for Lady Gubbins for the good manners she possessed because it was only then that she announced that 'the bloody dog' had peed in her boot! I thought it would make a good title for a play called *Lady Gubbins' Boot*.

We enjoyed social occasions with Lady Gubbins and her husband. Major-General Sir Colin Gubbins was almost a superhuman man who was physically very well-built. He was born and brought up on the Island of Mull and rose through the ranks in the army. Throughout the war he was head of SOE (Special Operations Executive) responsible for all the allied agents parachuted into France and Holland to help the resistance movement with arms and ammunition and organisation ready for D-Day. The general spoke six languages fluently, including being an interpreter in Russian, and at the outbreak of war was working with a Cambridge professor breaking Russian military codes. It was a rare gift that at a reunion of SOE personnel from so many different countries, he could, with a stiff gin in his hand, walk round the assembly room chatting with them in their native language.

Lady Gubbins was a very good cook and I don't think I have had a more delicious supper than her casseroled woodcock. The general was a very, very good shot and he would come over to Borve and shoot the woods with me when the woodcock were in and think nothing of getting a right and a left with both barrels of his shotgun, for which, in the old days, Bols Gin of Holland would issue a certificate and a prize of a bottle of Bols Gin. Not only was the general extremely clever but he was also very tough. Having come out of his flat in London and flown up to the Isle of Harris to his holiday cottage he would immediately don his filibeg (light-weight kilt) and be ready for action. On one occasion he fell into the bog at Borve and had quite a job escaping from the sodden peaty mess that he had fallen into but he shook himself like a dog with peat flying from his kilt, whereupon I said, 'Don't you think we ought to get back to the Lodge [we were only a mile or so from it] and you put a pair of my jeans on?' But he said we should carry on. He really was a 'toughy'. He had lost his first wife, and the current Lady Gubbins (in her broken English because she was a Norwegian by birth) said he had buried one wife and 'will soon be burying me' trying to keep up with him. She used to shoot with him; she too was a good shot and a wonderful woman.

I am sure that some of the strengths which the general possessed came from his ability to imbibe gin and water in equal quantities as a daily ration. When we had finished the day's shooting at Borve we would come back to the Lodge and have a drink and a light lunch before they went home. He always had gin with a dash of water and he would virtually finish a bottle of Gordons gin and be none the worse for it.

VISITORS

Quite a number of crofters with an energetic wife would offer bed-and-breakfast accommodation. In most cases the visitors who came proved to be quite harmless, nice quiet people, birdwatchers and fishermen and so on. But a great variety of people came and there had to be the odd rotten apple in the barrel-load.

The post office at Seilebost had a very energetic postmistress and she took in folk for bed and breakfast. Her husband was a good deal older than her but a wonderfully strong man who went on well into his 90s and was awarded an MBE for his work in the crofting community. He jealously guarded the grass in front of their post office as being a fruitful hay crop, well fenced off to avoid depredations by the sheep which were always wandering in the road looking for an easy bite for themselves and their lambs, but the post office had a good stone wall round the garden and this protected John Ferguson's precious hay crop providing winter feed for his one house cow. Well, sadly, a family arrived having booked the bed-and-breakfast and surprised John and his wife by bringing their pet Great Dane dog with them which Mrs Ferguson said they could let loose in the walled garden. When I met John at the end of the visitor's first week he was really cursing the 'bliddy' dog, saying that its paws were the size of gumboots and it had flattened his entire hay crop – so occasionally visitors came with an unwelcome accessory in the form of a huge dog.

As a matter of interest, on his 92nd birthday John Ferguson climbed the 1,000 foot-high hill together with the other shepherds to gather the sheep – he was a very, very fit man.

In the 1960s the influx of Pakistanis was just beginning; they found Stornoway a very acceptable place to live and start a business. Indeed they have, in fact, taken over virtually all the general stores in the town. In the 1960s Butta Mohammed ran a thriving haberdashery store in Stornoway and, like many Pakistanis, had a fairly large family. The eldest son bought himself a big suitcase and he would go in a little van all the way down to Harris as far as Rodel selling cheap shirts, underwear, ladies' blouses, etc., a whole heap of cotton goods imported from Pakistan and Bangladesh. Thanks to a sort of grapevine, Butta Mohammed would know when the shepherds in Harris, for example, were having one of their occasional sheep-gatherings on the hill. The 'darkies', as they were known in those days, knew the crofter women were alone in the house with the husband away on the hill so they would have a captive audience.

They would hump a heavy suitcase out of the van and walk across the bog, knock on the croft house door and very politely drop anchor there until the crofter's wife knew she had better buy something to get rid of them, so they would achieve a sale at most stopping points.

Many crofters' wives never went up to Stornoway. They bought a lot of their cotton vests or underwear by mail order from a catalogue, particularly the catalogue of J.D. Williams (always pronounced 'Jai-Dee' Williams) of Manchester, who would even send goods on approval all the way to the Hebrides. So there was a profitable seam to be exploited by the Pakistanis selling to a captive audience in their croft houses with only 'Jai-Dee' Williams suffering the subsequent loss in his catalogue business.

I happened to see this young Pakistani when he got out of his van at the gate at the end of our drive; he was staggering up the drive lugging his suitcase full of cotton goods. As I was out and about, I intercepted him as he was ringing the bell of the front door, accosting him before anybody answered the doorbell. I welcomed him and said, 'Do come in, and leave that blessed suitcase in the porch because I want to show you something that will probably save your life.' So, protesting, he came into the house with me. It was spring-time and in the main wing of the Lodge which we used to let there were four bedrooms on the ground floor and the inside of each bedroom was stacked high with wheelbarrows. I had been so pleased with a wheelbarrow that I had bought through mail order that I had written to the makers Wilmot's of Bristol offering to act as their sole agent for the Outer Isles. They were so attracted by the offer that they sent a good supply of wheelbarrows carriage-paid all the way to Borve Lodge in the Hebrides; it must have been a very innocent clerk who attended to my offer. A hundred wheelbarrows were stacked in these four bedrooms, just as they had arrived on a lorry at the port of Tarbert. It was my job to bolt them together to assemble them. So I said to the Pakistani, 'You are indeed very welcome and I will make a special discount to you in selling you one of these wheelbarrows with pneumatic tyres which will enable you to go to the croft houses across the bog without sinking into the bog with the heavy suitcase. You will be able to put the suitcase in the wheelbarrow, and think of the saving on your back muscles. The weight of the suitcase is far too heavy for you to be humping up and down the island, you need a barrow.'

'Oh, my goodness,' he said, 'I do not want a barrow.'

'Well,' I said, 'I am going to let you have it very reasonably, at a discounted price.' I didn't tell him that Wilmot's, on a £5 wheelbarrow, were giving me 33⅓ per cent discount and an extra 2½ per cent if I settled within a month of receiving them. Every crofter in Harris and Lewis had a good Wilmot's wheelbarrow and they blessed me twice over, but the Pakistani continued with his protestations: 'Oh, goodness me, I do not need a wheelbarrow.' Off he went backing down the drive still protesting that he did not need a wheelbarrow. I never saw him again; it was a wonderful way of defeating a keen salesman by trying to sell him something.

It is interesting to note that since those good old days, the Pakistani population of Stornoway has increased ten-fold, and they have made themselves thoroughly at home in spite of the 60 inches of rain a year clattering down in the grey streets of Stornoway, not noted for its sunshine hours.

Important visitors to the Lodge were Pat's and my parents. Both sets had frowned on our notion of making a living in the Hebrides but once they realised our youthful enthusiasm was going to conquer all, they warmed to the subject and really enjoyed coming to stay with us. My father made one proviso: even though he was 70 years of age, he was still mad keen on cricket, so the one condition of his coming all the way from Nottingham to holiday with us was that I should prepare a cricket pitch. So, having taken an early crop of hay off the grass between the Lodge and the seashore I got the lawnmower on the job and kept mowing a 22-yard strip, creating a useful pitch ready for my father's arrival. Of course, he didn't realise that cricket was unheard of in the Outer Hebrides, so when it came to making up a team, people like Lachlan MacLellan and Alec MacLennan plus other innocents, including the girls working in the Lodge, were recruited to form a modest cricket team and they all took a turn at bowling and batting. I felt my father was following in my tradition of 'empire-building', introducing cricket to the native inhabitants.

In spite of his failing eyesight I could never manage to bowl my father out. He stood there, with no pads on his legs, and I would send down the fastest balls that I could manage, but he was a very fine batsman – he had an eye for a ball like a hawk. However, he met his match when I put Lacky on to bowl. In spite of several summers of high endeavour Lacky never managed to release the ball with his hand above his shoulder, releasing the ball always too soon so it went up in the sky. He was a strong man so the cricket ball would go way up 20 or 30 feet and drop down almost on the head of my father who was waving his bat about trying to cope with the falling ball coming down like a bullet straight at his head! By a miracle, on one occasion the ball actually hit the stumps and there was a great yell: 'Out, Out, Out!' My father used to play top-class cricket so his embarrassment was almost too marvellous to behold! In fact, this proved to be a happy ending to his cricketing days because, suffering from a weak heart which affected the blood supply to his eyes, he eventually spent the last ten years of his life totally blind, looked after by a marvellous wife (who had also been a wonderful mother). My father was a splendid man and I was so happy that we could look back on those joyful days in Harris.

Amazingly, our visitors discovered certain attributes of the peaty water which we were drinking. It was coloured a faint brown caused by dissolved peat; these days it would be condemned by the health and safety people. The mains water had now been laid on to many crofts including the Lodge, but in the early days of which we are

Borve Lodge in 1955 north face, round garden with Borve House and original byre in the background.

talking, the water was quite natural with some dissolved peat particles in it which we assured our visitors was quite harmless. Mr Chinnery, my father-in-law's great friend whom he brought up to the Lodge for a holiday and who had had a lifetime tea-planting in Assam, suffered from a chronic form of dysentery. He found the water was therapeutic and after a stay of a month his dysentery disappeared not to return. He was so grateful, but it was nothing to do with us, it was the peaty water.

When we left Harris we went to live down south. My second daughter Joanna, as a teenager, developed minute warts all over her hands, which were very embarrassing as they were visible and irritating. But after leaving the Isles we continued to go back year after year for our holidays there, spending one month in Laxdale Cottage drinking water which was very peaty, piped from a wee lochan. We had to sieve the water as it was dark brown with peat, but we still drank it and in the course of the month's school holidays up there Jo lost all her warts; they just disappeared. So we should really be telling new tourists to buy some bottled peat water as a cure for warts and chronic dysentery!

In our early days visitors included Dr Jimmy Campbell and his wife Betty, from whom I learned a good deal about the different species of birds in the Hebrides. Jimmy's notes and records were sadly never published but over many years he contributed greatly to the knowledge of Hebridean birds. He carried with him the best telescope I have ever seen with which from the top of the cliff at Seilabost we could observe the different species of Scoter that assembled in the Sound of Taransay for their annual moulting in October. The telescope could also pick up Mr Campbell, the farmer owner of Taransay, as he sat reading a newspaper outside his house, and we could almost read the contents of the paper, such was its power. Betty, his wife, was intrigued because I was able to give her news of Sir John Gray, the Chief Justice of Zanzibar, who never took his leave in England, always going to South Africa. As Sir John was her uncle she was delighted to get first-hand news from me regarding his work in Zanzibar. The friendship with Jimmy Campbell lasted for many years till he died.

Another long-lasting friendship was struck up with a young man, Robin Andrew, who was a very knowledgeable and keen birdwatcher, with whom I continue to swap bird notes. I stayed with him many times in his home near Blairgowrie.

Early on in our years at Borve a young man who was on holiday in Tarbert, Harris called at the Lodge to explain that he was buying his way out of the Navy and was wanting to rent a cottage in Harris so that he could pursue his career as an artist. He had heard of our keeper's cottage at Laxdale and wondered if he might utilise it as his residence. He seemed an extremely nice man and as breeding goes he was one of the Gasks of Inverness, whose full name was Desmond Robin Walter Gask. So having agreed that he could have Laxdale Cottage at a peppercorn rent and that he would do various jobs to supplement the rent, he bought himself out with their lordships (of the Admiralty) two months later. He was conned into buying a souped-up Ford Prefect which pretended to be a second-hand estate car, complete with timber frame. He arrived in Harris with the car sagging under the weight of books, artists' materials, records, etc. Not surprisingly, as he climbed the cliff road at Seilebost on his way to report his safe arrival, he had the shock of seeing his front offside wheel going up the hill in front of him as the car veered off the road into the ditch. Luckily for him, the road gang under Angus MacDonald happened to be patching at the time. They all gathered and manually lifted the car back onto the road, kicking the mudguard to free the remaining front wheel. Sadly their muscular work showed that all the timber framework of this souped-up car was rotten and the top of the car came off!

He lived happily on his own in the cottage by Loch Laxdale, undeterred by the distance of seven miles from Tarbert, to where he would walk across the hills and back again to collect provisions from the shops. He was very useful, helping improve the cottage by, for example, laying on a polythene water pipe from a wee lochan up in the hill to give him some fresh water down in the cottage. He also planted and fenced a lovely copse of willow and aspen. Although a tiny bit of woodland it was highly attractive to a range of birds, including the cuckoos which would drive everyone mad in early summer. And at the Lodge he was very helpful with fencing, ditching and other odd jobs on the farm. After three or four years he informed me he was leaving, but left no forwarding address, and the last I heard of him was that he was working for British Rail in Edinburgh. I was sad to lose touch with him after a good stay in Harris.

HOTELS

In the fifties there were only two hotels on the island. By virtue of the location the Harris Hotel in Tarbert was far busier than the Rodel Hotel. The former was owned by Tommy Cameron and his wife Elizabeth, the building always immaculately maintained inside and out. The food was always reliable and the bar well stocked. Tommy in his tweeds and plus-fours was a most genial host. Fishing guests could enjoy the Laxadale lochs which provided mainly sea trout and a few salmon. The hotel bar trade was especially busy over the New Year. Whisky with a chaser of MacEwan's beer was the order of the day.

I usually called in on the day of the autumn cattle sale and on one occasion hung my new cap on a peg in the hall. Some months later I was getting prepared for the spring sale and I could not find my best cap at home. Imagine how delighted I was to find it was still on the peg in the hotel hall!

Rodel Hotel stands at the southern tip of the island on the edge of a sheltered harbour. Jock MacCallum was the owner and a perfect host. It was an old-fashioned hotel with a faithful clientele which included such illustrious characters as the Bishop of Zanzibar who spent a good slice of his home leave enjoying the fishing for salmon and sea trout which was owned by the hotel.

Good plain cooking always included a fish course and an excellent meat dish. The bedrooms were comfortable and the tariff reasonable. There was a large but very plain public bar at the rear which was presided over by both of Jock's brothers, Hughy and Callum, especially at peak times like New Year.

Occasional travellers were rare but very welcome. One gentleman who booked for a one-week stay asked Jock if it would be all right for him to visit friends in Stornoway at the weekend and leave his case in his bedroom because he looked forward to a second week in which to finish his writing assignment. Jock readily agreed, but when there was no sign of the guest returning by the following Wednesday, he took the liberty of checking on the contents of the heavy suitcase. He was shocked to discover a number of large stones carefully wrapped in newspaper!

Shortly after a two-page article appeared in the *Field* magazine under the heading 'The Last Stag in Harris', complete with sourced photo of the South Harris mountain Roneval. I do not know if the author's fee was used to pay the hotel bill. As the Scots say, 'I hae me doots.'

For some time the royal family enjoyed cruising via the Western Isles en route to Aberdeen and thence to Balmoral for their summer holiday. In August 1956 the Queen together with the Duke of Edinburgh and Princess Margaret landed at Rodel for a quick tour of Harris which included a visit to Mrs Macuish at Seilebost to see her at her loom weaving Harris Tweed. The royal visit is recorded in a plaque mounted on the east wall of the Rodel Hotel.

The MacCallum brothers augmented their income with petrol sales from their antique semi-rotary pump which slowly filled the glass vessel which was then released to put in another gallon. They were also sole suppliers of coal and anthracite which came from Greenock by a 'puffer'. Bar sales were boosted by 'Royal Household' whisky blended by Buchanan's and only available at Rodel and royal residences. (It was Buchanan's challenge to Johnnie Walker Black Label.)

THE BENEFITS
OF HOLIDAY VISITORS

Having decided that paying guests were no longer a paying proposition, we decided to let 'sporting quarters'. These were self-catering with the tenants buying their fresh food daily from our farm at retail prices. This enabled us to make a reasonable profit.

With a cottage down by the front gate at the drive entrance plus two wings of the Lodge, we found a ready response to an advertisement which we placed in the magazine the *Lady*. We chose this magazine because it regularly appeared in all the clubs in Britain's major cities and, also, it was popular for clubs in overseas countries.

One of the first families to respond to this advertisement offering sporting quarters, with salmon and sea trout fishing, was Dr Ian and Pat Jameson with their three children from Salisbury in Wiltshire. They arrived on a late ferry in early September and so they experienced the horror of driving on the narrow Harris roads cutting through the rocky hill country which lay between Tarbert, their port of arrival, and the west coast road to Borve, a total of fourteen miles.

View from eastern boundary of farm to Borve Lodge, Gate Cottage, the estuary and Sound of Taransay.

None of the hillocks had been levelled out when the road was made so the car headlights were shooting up skywards giving no indication of what lay ahead. No wonder the young children were frightened travelling through what almost looked like a moonscape, questioning their mother as to why on earth she had chosen such a country in which to have their summer holiday. However, after a really friendly welcome with a cup of tea and a fresh-made scone, they soon began to feel more at home in Borve Lodge.

At that time of year, we had around a dozen children of different ages all holidaying in the Lodge and the cottages. While Dr Jameson teamed up with his favourite ghillie, Lachlan MacLellan, and went off fishing for the day on Fincastle, I would fix other fishermen up with other fishing on different lochs. The children of these different families were always pleased to help me on the farm. A sample of their activities included hauling logs across the peat-bog from the wood where I had cut Sitka spruce or Douglas fir for use as gate posts or strainer posts for the fencing I was busy with. We would loop a heavy wagon rope round a seven-foot gatepost and with the tallest child at the front and smallest at the back, we would haul the

log over the smooth peat-bog as far as the main road, where I could get it onto a tractor-drawn trailer to take it to wherever it was to be set up for fencing.

After a day's activity hauling logs the children would be rewarded in different ways, one of the favourites being a byre cocktail party where I sat on my milking stool hand-milking our wonderful house cow Kuchi. The children all had their own log big or small to sit on against the byre wall telling stories and watching everything that I was doing. For the cocktail party they were

The new byre created from the garage, hayloft over, first used January 1959.

told to dress appropriately for the event, which meant that they all wore swimming costumes! One by one they came up towards the hind end of the cow and on the command 'open your mouth' they would open their mouths wide and I would spray a squeeze of milk directly into their mouths and then finish by spraying them up and down over their bodies. They would then run the hundred yards to the beach to swim the milk off! This became an annual event as families repeated their visits year after year.

These were the early days of barbeque. We would get a good fire going on the beach, and a great favourite amongst the children was dampers, a mixture of flour and water round the end of a stick. They would cook sausages and the dampers and even the odd wee brown trout that they had caught during the day.

Saturday nights we always played Scottish country dance records in the big, oak-floored sitting-room where, apart from me acting as DJ, everybody, children and all, learnt to Scottish country-dance to the music of Jimmy Shand and his band.

Dr Jameson's was one of the first families to stay at the Lodge and he and the family came back year after year. His eldest was a girl, Clodagh, and they called me down to their home in Salisbury to propose her toast at her 21st birthday party. Then when she married John Scott, a marine engineer, I was privileged to make the speech proposing the 'toast to the bride' at her wedding. Dr Jameson and his wife were so delightful a couple that Pat Jameson was godmother to our third daughter Caroline. After some years holidaying in Harris, the position of a doctor at the Harris practice became vacant and Dr Jameson so loved Harris that he abandoned his practice in Salisbury and took the position of GP in South Harris until he retired. If he was around on the Glorious Twelfth he and I would set off up the hill of Blaeval gradually gaining height, looking for the elusive grouse.

I remember one hot sunny day on the Twelfth Ian Jameson and I were climbing Blaeval; he was somewhat overweight and, sweating profusely, said, 'I will have to take a break and sit down, this climb is tiring me out' – but in true medical fashion he added, 'The dilation of my arteries is so powerful at the moment that it must be doing me a power of good.' I finally attended Dr Jameson's funeral and very reluctantly delivered the eulogy but I was affected greatly by the proximity of his coffin which carried his fishing rod and his deerstalker hat marking the joyful days that he had had with rod and gun in Harris. (Ian finally retired to a village in Norfolk to be near an old farming friend of his – he was buried in Norfolk, not in Harris.)

Of Ian's two sons the younger one, who was a very jolly youngster when sitting on his log in the byre, subsequently decided to take up acting as a career. He finally made his name with writing and producing the story of *Balamory* for children's television. The story was based around the town of Tobermory with its attractive painted houses on the Island of Mull. In fact, it really boosted the number of visitors going to the island to the point where some of the residents of that town got tired of answering questions being put to them by visitors as to where *Balamory* was based.

Clodagh emigrated with her husband to his native Australia and now lives on the Fraser river in Queensland where John was an engineer on board a coastal steamer.

I mention all this to give one example of mutual benefits derived from, one could say, an accidental friendship that brought so much pleasure to both our families and to Lachlan MacLellan who looked forward to his annual ghillying session.

Nearly all our visitors braved the elements and would go down to the beach and swim, but I had to warn them that if the sea was rather rough and the wind was in the west blowing straight onto the beach, they had to be very careful to avoid being caught by the strong undertow. One group of youngsters ignored this advice and were swimming in the surf; one of them got into difficulties, but in the nick of time friends pulled her out onto the shore and we had to hang her upside down to get rid of the water from her lungs. This was successful. Not a lesson that I wanted to learn more than once, but useful to know that hanging a person upside down, literally by the legs, is the best way of draining seawater out of the lungs.

WEATHER

Life at Borve was very dependent upon weather. I don't think I ever missed a weather forecast in the whole time we lived up there as the weather totally dominated one's thinking. Being on the edge of the Atlantic, the weather could change without warning.

I remember we decided to get the dinghy out into the water and with the Seagull outboard motor (for the purist a super 40+ with a long-reach propeller: simplicity itself, no need for a battery, just a rope pull for a starter) and, on a perfect morning, we manhandled the dinghy into the sea at Horgabost and loaded up for our four children, plus a nephew, plus food and tentage enough to last for a two-day visit to the island of Taransay. On arrival it was calm and sunny and we pitched the tents, all old stock, pre-war tentage. By the following morning the heavens had opened, a gale had sprung up from the south, and the children were howling because the tents were leaking like sieves. I had forgotten to load the supply of potatoes, but mercifully Pat had packed a good supply of porridge oats. The gale got worse and worse and the children were hanging on to the tent poles to stop them blowing away – it blew for 48 hours. Water was actually running down the grass bank and flowing under the tents. Pat was on her knees with a primus stove making porridge. On the third day the gale relented sufficiently for us to pack everything up into sodden heaps, much of which we abandoned and left where it was. We set off every child with its own load tied to its back carrying lamps and porridge oats, all the essentials. We headed eastwards at least a mile from the camping site to the old relic of a schoolhouse whose corrugated-iron roof was stuffed with old oilskins to stem the leaks. We found a dry spot to make our temporary home until such time as the gale abated sufficiently for us to sail the two miles back across the Sound of Harris to Horgabost.

At that time there was a black house on the island, occupied by an elderly lobster fisherman and his wife, Mr and Mrs MacRae. They took pity on us and braved the elements to walk for a quarter of a mile over to us with some fresh-baked scones. Their son, their only child Ewan, lived with them and went out with his father every day lobster-fishing. When he was in his late twenties, a nurse from the south of England staying at a bed-and-breakfast in Horgabost made friends with him when he brought the lobsters ashore and persuaded him to let her go out with him lobster-fishing. The inevitable occurred; they got married. She abandoned her nursing career and used to go out with him every day in his dinghy, lifting lobster pots, baiting the pots and putting them down, and then they would row back and have a late breakfast. Quite a tough life for a 'towny'!

It is worth noting that Ewan's father, old man MacRae, was still paid a very modest salary for being the postman for Taransay. He used to row across to Horgabost to the postbox there, pick up the post and then row it back to Taransay for his house and for the Campbell brothers who farmed the island. The Campbell brothers were living in an almost derelict farmhouse with wallpaper curling off the walls and filth everywhere. The senior brother Campbell was noted for his meanness, or, at best, some might call it thrift. He was still using two horses and a single-furrow plough to cultivate his small area of oats. One day the plough gave up the struggle and broke up, and old man Campbell came over to Horgabost and asked if anyone had a spare plough that he could buy. One of the Horgbost folk said, 'I think Mr Wilkinson at the Lodge has a single-furrow plough, I have seen it when I have been over there. Maybe he would let you have it.'

So old Campbell came over to the Lodge, almost begging. He said he heard that I had got a plough and could he have a look at it. I said, 'By all means, but it is almost a museum piece, and at the moment it is lying half buried in a sand dune covered in rust and I have no use for it at all.'

Nevertheless I took him over to the plough and he got hold of the handles – the handles had long since rusted – and the mould-board was totally rusted and partially perforated. He stood by the plough and true to his thrift he started criticising it, saying that the handles had gone.

I said, 'Something has to go as you get older.'

And then he said, 'Look at the mould-board, it is in a terrible state.'

I replied, 'Well, don't carry on with this criticism, it is not for sale. Somebody has dumped it in the sand-dune and it not worth anything. If it is of any use to you, take it for nothing.' However, on more mature consideration he decided that nothing could be done to reclaim it and, still grumbling, went away having drawn a blank.

He was not a poor man; when he took 200 lambs to market and got help in getting them to Tarbert from where they were shipped to the mainland, he hired a wee local boy Douglas (wee Dougie) as the one and only helper. He and Dougie went on the ferry boat across to the mainland with these 200 lambs; they had an excellent high tea on board the MacBrayne's ferry on the way over and when the waiter came with the bill, he made it out for both Campbell and wee Dougie, but Campbell insisted that the wee boy would pay for his own. He had already given the boy a small sum towards subsistence so he insisted on the wee boy paying his own bill for his first supper on board the ferry.

Occasionally hurricane-force winds would come across the Atlantic and reach Force 12 – a wind so strong that I was unable to stand up in it. One day, December 12, 1956 Stornaway recorded 110mph for 24 hours when a Force 12 blew, it took the flat corrugated-iron roof off the poultry house and in one gust blew it across the machair and lodged it upright in one piece against the wall of the Lodge, 200 yards away. The 50 hens which were housed in it were sucked out and blown across the estuary, the gale holding them very firmly against the sandbank in the marram grass. It took the whole morning for Alastair and me on our knees dragging an empty poultry crate between us to gather up the hens one by one. And having filled the crate with a dozen birds we then dragged it up the estuary to the safety of the Lodge, emptied the crate and went back for another load. Standing up was absolutely impossible; we had to move on our knees. It is not surprising that after nearly ten years of this sort of life any sense of heroism was lost and it dawned on me that I was just being an idiot carrying on with it.

RELIGIOUS OBSERVANCE

The crofters are very keen on their religious observance and Sunday, the Sabbath, is treated with great respect whatever the denomination. No crofter worth his salt will undertake any outside work on a Sunday and when you think of the highly physical nature of his work for six days of the week, it only seems most sensible to allow the body to rest on the Sabbath. Churchgoing is either once or twice on a Sunday and the churchgoers are divided between the Church of Scotland and the Free Presbyterian Church. Even visiting one's close relations on a Sunday is frowned upon. The day must be given over to Bible-reading, prayer and churchgoing. I achieved a notice in the *Stornoway Gazette* when, after a month of continuous wet days, Sunday was a gloriously sunny and windy day – perfect for drying hay. So when midnight struck, I went out until 8 a.m. and with the tractor and trailer I carted the cocks of hay that had been lying out for a month (but had been kept dry because of the technique of cocking) and I managed to gather it and stack it into the hayloft, pitching it up single-handedly. I finally went to bed, exhausted, at 9 a.m. The *Stornoway Gazette* noted that one Sassenach in Harris kept the Sabbath observance but after midnight carted all his hay in the one dry spell of the week!

At the Lodge we were lucky to have among our summer visitors several good churchmen who came every year on holiday. They organised our own little service of worship on a Sunday in the big room at the Lodge and made up their own prayers. We had enough hymn-books to go round and we often had as many as 20 for the service. In an appendix to this book there is a prayer that Dr Jameson produced for use in our holiday services.

Funerals were conducted on the west side of the island, or at least the burial took place on the west side in two or three quite large cemeteries, because on the east side the soil was so shallow and so rocky that it was not possible to bury the dead, so the cemeteries were on the west side, on the machair. Indeed, before motorised transport became available, the coffins were brought over the hills from the east to the west coast on certain well-marked tracks and to this day the small cairns are still visible at roughly quarter of a mile apart where the coffin-bearers rested the coffin on the stone cairns on their way over. Usually six strong men carried the coffin by its handles on either side until they got to the western burial ground. The distance of the main cairn-marked routes was usually about three miles. The tradition to this day at a funeral is that the menfolk will carry the coffin and they will keep taking it in turns until all the male mourners have had a turn at carrying the coffin before it is put into the hearse to be driven to the cemetery. At the cemetery the grave would already have been dug and prepared and the near male relatives of the deceased lower the coffin with its attached cords gently into the grave, and then they all take it in turns to push some soil in on top of the coffin.

Religious observance by the population does mean that they have a code of conduct in the Bible with its Ten Commandments to live by, and so crime in the island and immoral behaviour are rare. The church services are all conducted in Gaelic and the singing mainly of the psalms is very distinctive in its form and music. An elderly member of the congregation will be the recognised leader and he is somewhat akin to a tuning fork: he will strike the right note and then men and women will follow with chanting a psalm. None of the Anglican Church hymns enter into the service.

Weddings are memorable affairs, particularly the celebratory ceilidh after the wedding when the groom's house will be just packed with people. I remember one wedding that I attended when the groom's house was so packed that there were guests clustered on a bed occupied by the groom's bedridden mother, who was not accustomed to having her bedroom invaded!

With both weddings and funerals, the guests and the mourners treat both with suitable respect. At a funeral, whilst the coffin is being carried out of the house, it is permitted for crofters to exchange a word or two on how the lambing is going or how the hay crop is shaping up, before coming smartly to attention when the coffin passes and taking a turn at carrying it – so it is not all doom and gloom!

BIRD-LIFE

All this time I did not neglect my great love of birdwatching and I kept a diary giving details of resident birds and particularly the migratory species (see the booklet *A Bird Watcher in the Isle of Harris*). As I mentioned before, the odd rarity would appear when least expected, such as the Little Auk washed up dead on the beach at Seal Bay.

The island of St Kilda is famous for its wildlife, but particularly for its Gannet colony. During the winter months the gannets disappear and travel well out to sea and down to southern oceans, but it is a good harbinger of spring to see them returning to the Sound of Harris, diving for the herring and other fish that they spear with their beaks to take back for their young on the rock stacks of St Kilda. They are indeed noble creatures.

In the period under review, various important changes took place, notably the introduction of organo-chlorine pesticides, particularly in the new sheep dips. Dieldrin was the wonder chemical which more or less obliterated the fly population throughout Britain. In particular, it affected the Hebridean breeding population of flies. In the early 1960s you could easily be covered in flies just walking about. I remember going to a funeral at Luskentyre, and there was a bald-headed man standing by the graveside and I thought he had a wig on as there were so many black flies settled on his bald pate that they completely covered it. Many of these flies were breeding in rotting seaweed on the seashore. This is no longer the case. The fly menace has largely disappeared such is the long staying power of a chemical like that. For a year or two the biting horseflies, or clegs as we call them in Harris, had seemingly been wiped out and it has taken quite a number of years for them to come back. During a hot spell they would bite the teats of a cow like Kuchi drawing blood and causing great irritation.

In the 1960s of a winter's evening I would watch Hooded Crows assembling together before flying, as a flock, to roost in the few trees that were to be found at Borve and at Horgabost. There would be a flock of perhaps 30 going off to roost together having spent the day fossicking on the beach and feeding on a dead sheep – there was always a dead sheep somewhere and the 'hoodies' would act like vultures and virtually clear them up. They were assisted in this scavenging by quite a useful number of Ravens. After a time the numbers of Hooded Crows and Ravens went into decline as they were not keen on feeding on the carcass of a sheep that had died on the hill as it was so impregnated with pesticide residues.

It was perhaps merciful that an examination of the nest of a pair of Golden Eagles which nested every year in an eyrie on a hillside in North Harris showed that the main food they had been giving their chicks was no longer carrion obtained from the carcass of a dead sheep but that salmon formed a major element of their diet. The eagles had become adept at watching the rivers for any salmon that were locked into a pool unable to go further upstream because the spate had died.

As the proprietor of good fishing in South Harris, part of my work was to prevent poaching of salmon and sea trout and, indeed, if I had been guilty of poaching in the Outer Hebrides, word would have spread like wildfire condemning me for such behaviour. However, when my wife and I went to visit a friend living in central Scotland who was a keen birdwatcher, he said, 'We will take a walk and follow the burn up the hill, it is only a small burn and when we get to the top, we shall see the Peregrine Falcons nesting there.' So my host led the way and I followed, and way behind our two wives and his two children followed more slowly. When we were well up the hill following the burn, we saw that there had not been enough rain to take the salmon all the way up to their spawning grounds. One salmon had developed fungus on its head; this type of fungus develops in salt water and when the salmon are delayed in getting to fresh water it spreads to the body. This pool was about the length of a cricket pitch and the salmon, size about five pounds, was 'to-ing' and 'fro-ing' watching us up on the bank of the brook and obviously scared.

I said to my host, 'There is nobody around and this poor salmon is suffering from this fungus and without getting you involved I will put it out of its misery.' So I picked up a stone from the river-bed and I hurled it at the fish. I knew when the stone left my hand that it would hit the target fair and square, and it hit the salmon on the back of the head and killed it. I was wearing gumboots, so I waded in and got it by the gills and brought it out. Fearful that somebody might have seen me poaching salmon, I did a poacher's trick of putting the salmon down my trouser-leg and hanging on to the tail with my right hand so that the salmon was invisible, except that I looked a bit awkward with one hand down my trouser-leg, but we walked on innocently for another hundred yards.

I have not got a good memory for dates but happily the Wimbledon men's final was on that day – I remember it was Pat Cash who won the match and we got home in time to see the final. On our way back, we had passed our wives and his children and we just said we were anxious to get back to watch the men's final on TV. The wives knew we were keen on tennis so they accepted that as an excuse for a quick return, unaware I was carrying contraband in my trousers. By a miracle I had brought two bottles of white wine almost in preparation for a salmon supper! So, having got the salmon into the larder before the ladies returned, we were able to tell my hostess that we had got a salmon for supper and no questions asked please, so we sat down to a five-pound salmon and a couple of bottles of excellent white wine to go with it, and we had seen Pat Cash winning the men's singles; it was a bit of a gala day! And the only time I had ever poached a salmon in my life.

In the 1960s when flies and insect life were still plentiful, there was a much more varied bird-life as a result, e.g. every summer's evening a flock of Common Gulls would feed amongst the grass between the Lodge and the sea – probably as many as a hundred gulls flitting amongst the tall grass catching moths. In fact, in the bird book which I have written giving details of the birds of Harris I have done a drawing of the common gulls feeding on moths at midnight, and they look like white fairies flitting to and fro in the long grass I had shut up for hay. The pesticide Dieldrin led to the reduction in flies and moths and all creepy crawlies and before the chemical got a grip on insect populations, Lapwings were quite common nesting on the machair land with its plentiful supply of insect life for feeding the lapwing chicks. Corncrake need good insect life for feeding their young and they were much more frequently heard in the old days. They are just beginning to come back in numbers now (2011).

A lot of species that have virtually become extinct on mainland Britain still find more feed for their young in the Hebrides, e.g. Cuckoos are still more plentiful in Harris than anywhere on the mainland. Other changes that are not connected with the insect life have occurred in the period under review; notably when we first went to the Isle of Harris, resident Greylag geese were unknown but now there are Greylags nesting in several favoured spots on the island. For more information on birds see my aforementioned book.

A Bird Watcher in the Isle of Harris

Notes and Records
1954-1963 & 1970-1995

by
Geoffrey D Wilkinson

Available from The Harris Tweed Shop, Main Street, Tarbert, Harris.

Price £3.00

CROFTERS' CLOTHES

Mindful of the fact that 60 inches of rain was not an uncommon annual rainfall over most of Harris, it is not surprising that the one essential item of dress was a pair of sound gumboots and the most popular were the most expensive because of their high rubber content, rejoicing in the splendid name of 'Hoods Bullseye'. For tramping the hill, gathering sheep and for on-croft work, the boots were turned down about four–five inches from the top, making walking much easier and providing a cushion for the calf.

The crofters' wives liked to have a home-knitted jersey to wear and during the summer months they would often milk their house cow squatting out in the pasture oblivious to whatever the weather threw at them.

On the Sabbath the men wore a suitably sober suit and the ladies similar, but adding a well-chosen hat purchased through a recent mail-order catalogue.

SUSTAINABILITY

A favourite topic these days is called 'sustainability' – that is to have a system of farming where external inputs are limited to those which are absolutely essential. On the farm at Borve I managed to grow sufficient basic crops to meet the needs of the small herd which increased year by year until we reached 15 breeding cows. Kuchi, the Shorthorn x Ayrshire, was a great example of sustainability. I bought her as a ten-year-old; she then produced a calf a year until old age overtook her and she went for slaughter, aged 16. As with all the other cows she seemed to thrive on the short and sweet summer pastures of the machair and then in the winter like the rest she had a daily ration of two or three sheaves of oats together with about half a stone (seven pounds) of chopped turnips and about ten pounds of June-made hay. I had to break the organic rules by treating her whenever the incipient mastitis flared up, usually when the weather turned colder, and an intra-mammary injection of penicillin was a necessity to get the mastitis under control. Trixie, an early purchase as a weaned calf from Quidnish, decided to have a serious go of pneumonia, but dosing her with an intra-muscular injection of Distaquin penicillin and a second dose the next day and covering her up with bags to keep her warm did the trick and she made a sound recovery never to be bothered with the illness again.

As with livestock, so with cropping. I could do nothing organically to counter the devastating effect of cabbage root maggot fly which every year attacked the seedling turnips. The fly would lay its eggs in the crown of the turnip and the maggots which hatched out would eat the heart out of the turnip, leading to complete loss of crop. Much as I disliked using powerful pesticides, I found the only way to save the crop was to spray it with DDT wettable powder. I was always learning something fresh about pests in an isolated place like the Outer Isles, that if they could not get cabbage to lay their eggs on they would be very satisfied with a crop of turnips!

Some research was needed with the gooseberry sawfly whose caterpillars decimated the foliage of the gooseberry bushes – it turned out that their alternate host on which they overwinter is the common rush of which there was a big crop in the marshy ground of the next-door neighbour's croft. I had to use DDT once again to get any sort of a crop.

Ideal suckler - Shorthorn cross Highland heifer, peat bog is visible in the background.

It was at this time that more powerful dips were being used to control certain pests of sheep and this was very effectively done with organo-chlorine pesticides, so effective that the sheep blowfly virtually became extinct after only a few years of using the powerful new insecticides.

The small oats *Avena strigosa* were a blessing although they did not produce a big crop; nevertheless it was a healthy one. Even the most common weed in the arable land, which was charlock, I never worried about spraying because it did a useful job as a stiff-stemmed weed acting as a prop to the oats which might easily have gone flat with the gales and rain which sometimes affected them in the summer.

The best land on the farm for cropping lay in the park across the main road where the mixture of peaty soil and the sandy machair would produce a useful crop of oats or turnips without much artificial manure, but on the machair itself I always needed to top up the basic seaweed manure with a touch of nitrogen and superphosphate, as the mineral status of the machair is so poor, it being a straight shell-sand in its origin.

When I now look back upon the development on the farm, I tend to forget how my one helper, Alastair MacLennan, and I had to mix the farming in with putting new ceilings in the bedrooms of the Lodge, how we drained the underground boiler area, how we cleared literally a mountain of rubbish from behind the cottage by the gate where over the years successive tenants had just dumped their household rubbish at the back of the cottage creating a mound of old gumboots, old tin cans, etc., you name it and it was there. We would take trailer-loads of rubbish along the cliff road, a one-mile haul, and tip this rubbish down a hundred-foot drop into a gorge which the Atlantic swell washed out on the high tide every day.

Alec and Alistair secure the hay cocks with herring netting.

SADNESS AND JOY

July 25, 1958: On the previous day the Luskentyre shepherds had been out on the hills gathering their sheep; all went well until on arrival at the fank there was no sign of Donald MacLeod who late in life had married Rachel Morrison. Donald was a very skilled builder who would contract to build a croft house and do the entire job himself, including plumbing and electrical work. One or two houses each year were his limit. Rumour had it that he was being pursued by the Inland Revenue on his tax affairs and that he worried so much that he decided to take his own life.

Such was the enormous respect for Donald, and his wife Rachel, that every able-bodied man turned out on the twenty-fifth to form a human chain which quartered the hill from Horsaclett right along to the western tip of Ben Luskentyre. About 200 men took part and sadly Donald's cap was the only item found of any significance on the edge of steep cliffs overlooking West Loch Tarbert.

1956: Jane Patricia born.

1958: Susan Joanna born.

1959: Caroline Sarah born.

1961: Heather Anne born.

After five years of earnest effort there was no sign of a pregnancy occurring, so encouraged by our proximity to civilisation after years in Africa we plucked up courage and decided to submit ourselves to fertility tests. I volunteered to go first and travelled on an early train up to London to attend a specialist fertility clinic in Harley Street. Happily the tests proved that my fertility was high, with sperms racing all over the place. Having squared a very handsome fee with the consultant, I went back to our temporary home with my parents-in-law in Sussex, where Pat was lucky enough to be looked after by an excellent gynaecologist at St Christopher's Hospital in Chichester. After minor surgery all was well, so we were delighted when we learned that Jane was expected. As a precaution, it was decided she should go over to Raigmore Hospital in Inverness when the time came to deliver the babe. All went splendidly and I caught a small

Pat with Jane in 1956.

plane, a de Havilland Heron, and in thick fog descended upon Dalcross Airport with the aid of only a radio beam (there was no radar guidance at that time). I realised then that a woman looks at her most beautiful when the first-born arrives.

The other daughters, Joanna, Caroline and Heather, arrived in fairly rapid succession and all were born in the Lewis Hospital at Stornoway. Pat always enjoyed going up there to have a babe, especially when she usually had two or three days in a preparatory ward to relax before delivery. The arrival of the fourth daughter, Heather, didn't allow this luxury. She arrived within minutes of us reaching the hospital after a 50-mile drive by Land Rover on a single-track road. Pat was suitably phlegmatic and complained she had missed out on the few days of rest before the birth – something she would have appreciated with three young ones already at home.

This is an opportunity to acknowledge the wonderful work performed for many years at the Lewis hospital by Dr Norman Jamieson who was the most capable general surgeon I have ever known. He would cope with trawlermen brought into Stornoway harbour with broken limbs after an accident at sea and he was also capable of doing complex brain operations. We were very lucky to have such a brilliant medical officer in charge of the hospital. He was ably supported in his work by Dr Jack Greig, who by coincidence also waited for six years for the arrival of his first-born. He and his wife named the babe Patience. They were subsequently our life-long friends.

In view of the sudden increase in our family numbers and the fact that we were always busy with holiday visitors, we put an advertisement into the *Scotsman* paper asking for help in the Hebrides with family and farm. We had 50 applicants, ranging from a lady in Bristol who was recovering from a nervous breakdown whose doctor had recommended a good break in isolation for recovery, to a retired male petty officer from the Navy who declared he was equally good with farm work and with children! The final result was that we employed two lovely girls: Sue Haslett, who had had enough of London life and came and spent very nearly a full year with us; and for a shorter stay, Carole Melville, a student from Edinburgh, who came for part of her gap year. It was a hard learning curve in certain respects. Sue was almost allergic to feathers, but I rapidly cured that one when we were working with the poultry. I threw a hen to her and said 'catch this'. She had no alternative but to catch it and was cured from then on! Carole spent more time with the children, especially Caroline who was a toddler. I am still in touch with both Sue and Carole.

Borve was a perfect place for bringing up children and I soon had Jane leading our first calf, Trixie, on a halter, taking her down to the river for a drink. It was then that I learned that my experience worldwide with cattle of many different breeds led me to believe that cattle regarded children quite differently from adults. Whether it was Jane with Trixie or Masai children in Africa looking after a herd of two or three hundred head, it was always amazing the respect which adult cattle gave to children.

The two oldest children, Jane and Jo, went to Seilebost Primary School and had an excellent grounding from Mrs MacLean, who coped wonderfully well with with 25 children of different ages from Reception to Year 6. Jo sat at a shared desk with Finlay MacLennan and very pleasingly her eldest son is named Finlay.

Readers will note that there is no further mention of the two younger daughters because after ten years on the island I decided that we must reluctantly seek greener pastures. There are many reasons for this decision, first among them being our determination that our children should experience the kind of education which both Pat and I had had; not necessarily enjoyable, but a very sound preparation for all that the world can throw at young people. Our income from the farm and summer visitors enabled us to make a small profit but in no way was it adequate to meet the educational needs we had in mind. Add to this the fact that farming in the Isles with a rainfall of very nearly 60 inches a year on poor hungry soils was not sustainable in the long run on a small acreage. Our herd of 15 breeding cows, self-supporting in every way, was the maximum the land or I could sustain. The physical labour involved with that size of herd, plus visitors, plus managing a Harris Tweed co-operative, was too demanding and I was aware that the same amount of energy in a job on the mainland would yield ten times the income. Because I'd done so much with young visitors I decided to train as a teacher and went down south to take a Postgraduate Certificate in Education, and from then on a new career developed.

Geoff with Caroline, Jane and Joanna in the round garden. Yellow Lab Dilly.

APPENDIX I

Loch Cistavat, Borve Lodge Farm – species identified by Dr Tom Warwick, Department of Zoology, University of Edinburgh, 1960

Plants:
Litorella uniflora – grows on the bottom with stiff cylindrical leaves, pointed at the top
Myriophyllum spicatum (Water milfoil) – feathery water weed, soft texture
Caltha palustris (marsh marigold)
Plantago maritima
Triglochin maritima
Chara vulgaris – a species of algae, harsh to the touch; an underwater plant

Animals:
Small damsel dragonfly, blue and black banding
Small snail *Potamopyrgus jenkonsi* (parthenogenetic)
Lymnaea peregra – host for liver fluke
Gammarus duebeni – a shrimp
Hydrobia jenkinsi – a common snail
Corixa scotti (water boatman)
Loch Leven trout – pink-fleshed (stocked in the past?)

Analysis of Loch Cistavat water:
Chlorine – 124mg per 1,000cc. This is about 1/150 the chlorine content of pure seawater so the water is really very fresh.
Calcium – 26mg per 1,000cc.

APPENDIX II
Prices as per 1960

A Massey Ferguson 35 diesel tractor bought new and delivered to Harris for the sum of £630.
A Ferguson mounted mower delivered to Harris was £110.
A new short-wheelbase Land Rover, petrol model, was £650.
A bottle of whisky was 38 shillings (£1.90). A bottle of sherry 25 shillings (£1.25).
Erinmore Flake pipe tobacco (I smoked 4 ounces a week) was 4 shillings (20p) an ounce. Cigarettes were 3 shillings and 10 pence (c. 19p) for 20.
Petrol 4 shillings (20p) per gallon.
The average wage in the United Kingdom was £9 10s (£9.50) per week.

APPENDIX III

Livestock Outputs

Suckled Calves sold at auction in September sales average weight 3–4 cwt:

	No.	Stot	Heifer
1956	4	2	2
1957	5	4	1
1958	6	5	1
1959	7	5	2
1960	12	11	1
1961	9	7	2
1962	15	7	8

Overall average net price £20 per head.

2 house cows maintained to provide all milk requirements for summer visitors and family.

Suckler cows – housed January to March, fed on 1 ton hay, small oats in sheaf, Bortfelder turnips chopped, all grown on farm.

Other Outputs

Vegetables and fruit – quarter of an acre devoted to carrots, peas, lettuce, gooseberries and strawberries for sale to visitors.

Early potatoes – sold in small lots to shops in Leverburgh, Tarbert and Stornoway. All seed boxed and chitted to ensure harvesting in June/July.

Eggs – 50 Rhode Island Red x Light Sussex hens kept on deep litter.

Eggs sold on contract to Lewis hospital and summer visitors.

Litter composed of peat dust, wood shavings and sawdust. A paraffin pressure lamp was used to provide additional light in winter to make a 14-hour day.

Eggs sent by public service bus to Stornoway in wooden egg box (locked).

Fishings – all fish caught on wet fly. Boats maintained on Lochs Fincastle, Laxdale, Sluice, Lackalee, Creaval and Manish. Ghillie compulsory for Fincastle and Laxdale.

Ten-year average annual basket 22 Salmon and 84 Sea Trout.

Salmon averaged 5–6lb. Sea Trout 1½lb.

All boats under cover for the winter all painted for new season.

Season ends 31 October.

APPENDIX IV

History of Borve Estate

1885 Estate owned by 7th Earl of Dunmore.

1885/6 Mr James Coward, tenant.

1887/1902 Lt.-Colonel George Percy, tenant.

1907 8th Earl of Dunmore.

1911 Enlargement of Borve Lodge. Viscount Leverhulme purchased the estate for £26,000 using Borve Lodge as his summer residence.

1922 Lord Leverhulme's guests shot 379 snipe, 104 woodcock, 10 stags.

1923 Lord Leverhulme completed new wing at Borve Lodge and built the round garden and improved outbuildings.

1925 Lord Leverhulme died. Borve Estate of 12,720 acres purchased by Mr Fradgley in 1927.

1933 Bought by Department of Agriculture for Scotland.

1934 Tenancy inherited by Miss Fradgley who ran the Lodge as an angler's hotel for one season.

1936 Department of Agriculture created numerous crofts with common grazings and sold off Borve Lodge with its 115 acres and sporting rights to Lt.-Colonel John Douglas Glen Walker.

26 May 1954 Col. Walker died aged 82 years, leaving his estate to his wife Kathleen Walker.

1955 Borve Estate purchased by Mr and Mrs Geoffrey Wilkinson, plus additional fishings of Lackalee and Creaval from the Horsaclett Estate.

1956–63 The Wilkinsons developed farming enterprise, letting sporting quarters with fishings to numerous tenants – average annual basket of 22 salmon and 184 sea trout.

1964 The Honourable Mrs Jean Cormack bought Borve and engaged Tony Scherr to manage and develop the fishery, resulting in the annual salmon catch increasing to 40 per season.

1977 Borve Estate sold to Highlands and Islands Development Board.

1984 Bought by Dr David Horrobin, who died in 2003.

APPENDIX V

A poem by David Griffiths from his collection dated 2007

'Don't Give Them Names' (Orphan lambs)

Don't give them names however sweet they are
And Spot and Smudge and Snowball may be apt
It may be touching that they bleat and run
To meet you when you shout 'It's breakfast time!'
Or 'Come and get it now!' and wag their tails
And butt the teat as if it were their dam.
Remember that you are not just their friend
You are their mother, father and their God
(That is if lamb's beliefs should stretch that far)
But, I advise you, do not give them names
For, giving names imparts a different role
Far, far beyond the keeping of a flock;
It signals trust and loyalty to them.
No turning back whatever ills there are
As it might be if men in overalls,
Snow-white like angels come to deal out Death
Your little charges would look back to you
With trusting eyes once more to rescue them
And you can only turn away and cry.
So you must see, no names however apt
For on a funeral pyre it's best that they
(For all concerned) remain anonymous.

APPENDIX VI

A Holiday Prayer used by Dr Ian Jameson at our Sunday service in the big sitting-room in Borve Lodge.

O God whose strength and beauty are shown in the glory and grandeur of Thy creation, be with us and bless us as on holiday we seek recreation and rest from daily toil.
May the beauty of nature reveal to us Thy beauty, the calm of the sea Thy peace, the majesty of the hills Thy strength, the warmth of the sun Thy love. Let no sinful or selfish thought or action spoil this time of rest for us or for others but rejoicing in Thy goodness, relaxing in Thy presence and responding to Thy love, may we find recreation of body, mind and spirit wherewith we may serve thee more faithfully in the tasks to which we shall return.
Through Jesus Christ our Lord
Amen

APPENDIX VII

Diagram cross-section of Fincastle dam wall

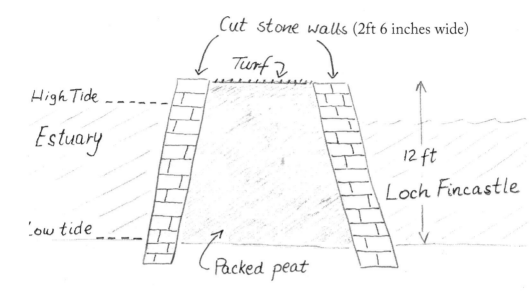

Cut stone walls (2ft 6 inches wide)

Turf

High Tide

Estuary

12 ft

Loch Fincastle

Low tide

Packed peat

GLOSSARY

TUP: Ram changed every 2 years to avoid inbreeding.

ELD EWE: A barren ewe.

WEDDER LAMB: A castrated lamb.

RAM LAMB: An entire male lamb.

EWE LAMB: Female lamb.

HOGGS: Ewe lambs after weaning.

TEGS: Weaned lambs in first winter.

KEDS: *Melophagus ovis* (false lice).

2-YR AND 3-YR-OLD WEDDERS: Used to be kept with the ewes on the common grazing, they would scrape through thick snow opening up heather and grass for the ewes. Later providing top-quality mutton.

SOUMING: A statement of the numbers and type of stock that a crofter is entitled to put on the common grazing.

INBYE LAND: Usually the land attached to the croft house for the exclusive use of the owner.

THE MACHAIR: The narrow belt of shell-sand soil forming the west coast of the island. Highly alkaline, pH 8.5, very short of necessary trace elements especially manganese, cobalt, iron, etc. If sheep grazed for too long on the machair they 'pine' for lack of cobalt and die. Moving them to browse heather and hill grasses rectifies the deficiency.

PEAT: Accumulation of sphagnum moss growing on an impervious base, e.g. Lewisian gneiss. Highly acid, pH 3.5.

PARR: A young salmon.

SMOLT: A young salmon, next stage.

FINNOCK: Young sea trout.

GRILSE: A young salmon that has been to sea once.

KELT: A mature salmon after spawning.

MESSAGES: Shopping.

MIDDEN: Dung-heap.

STOT: Young ox. A castrated male.

STOB: Fencing stake.

STRATH: Broad valley.

DUIN: Fort.

SLAINTE MHATH (SLANGEVAR): Good Health (a Gaelic toast).

BODACH: an old man (Gaelic).

CAILLEACH: an old woman (Gaelic).

CEILIDH: social gathering (Gaelic).

BIBLIOGRAPHY

Boddington, David (2010) *St Kilda Diary* The Islands Book Trust

Boyd, J. Morton and Boyd, Ian L. (1990) *The Hebrides* (New Naturalist No. 76)

Cunningham, W.A.J. (1983) *Birds of the Outer Hebrides* Perth, Methuen

Duncan, Angus (2005) *Hebridean Island Memories of Scarp* Edinburgh, Birlinn Ltd

Fraser Darling, F. (1955) *West Highland Survey* Oxford, Oxford University Press

Fraser Darling, F. (1944) *Island Farm* London, Bell

Fraser Darling, F. (1940) *Island Years* London, Bell

Fraser Darling, F. (1947) *Natural History in the Highlands and Islands* (New Naturalist No. 6)

Hunter, Janet (2001) *Islanders and the Orb* Stornoway, Acair Ltd

Hutchinson, Roger (2008) *The Soap Man* Edinburgh, Birlinn Ltd

Johnson, Alison (1998) *A House by the Shore* Time Warner

Keble Martin, W. (1965) *The Concise British Flora* Ebury Press & Michael Joseph

Lawson, Bill (2002) *Harris in History and Legend* Edinburgh, Birlinn Ltd

Lawson, Bill (1991) *St Clement's Church at Rodel* Northton, Harris

Lawson, Bill (1993) *The Teampull at Northton and the Church at Scarista* Northton, Harris

Love, John A. (2009) *A Natural History of St Kilda* Edinburgh, Birlinn Ltd

MacDonald, Finlay J. (1985) *Crotal and White* London, Futura

MacDonald, Finlay J. (1985) *The Corncrake and the Lysander* London, Futura

MacDonald, Finlay (1985) *Crowdie and Cream* London, Futura

MacKenzie, David (1954) *Farmer in the Western Isles* London, Faber & Faber Ltd

MacKenzie, W. C. (1919) *The Book of the Lews* Paisley, A. Gardner

Nicolson, Nigel (1960) *Lord of the Isles* London, Weidenfeld & Nicolson

Ralph, R. (ed.) (1996) *MacGillivray William, A Hebridean Naturalist's Journal 1817/1818* Stornoway, Acair Ltd

Stuart, Hamish (1916) *The Book of the Sea Trout* London, Martin Secker

Vogler, Gisela (2002) *A Harris Way of Life* Stornoway, *Stornoway Gazette Ltd*

Wilkinson, Geoffrey (2002) *Bird Watcher in the Isle of Harris* Private Publication

Other Sources:

Blacks Veterinary Dictionary (1928)

Fenton, A. *The Island Blackhouse – A Guide to No. 42 Arnol, Lewis* (1978) pub. by HMSO, Edinburgh

Western Isles Tourist Association *The Western Isles – Official Guide Book*

ACKNOWLEDGEMENTS

Bonny Sheppard-Jones for her patience and skill in typing the manuscript.

Rita Brass for her initial input.

Carole Michele Cox for her constant encouragement.

David Griffiths for his permission to print his poem 'Don't Give Them Names'.

Tony Scherr for much assistance.

John Sheppard-Jones for his help and input.

Machair cropping-potatoes with small oats with Taransay and North Harris hills in the background.

Borve Lodge 1960. East face with Caroline and Carole Melville.

Bleaval
398m.

-S

COMMON
NG

SCARISTAVORE
COMMON GRAZING

Borvebeg
sheep
Fank

INBYE LAND

Pinus
contorta

John
MacDodd

Loch an Duin

Neil
Morrison

Scarista
PO

Finlay
MacKenzie

Angus
MacSween

Iris
& Bog

Danny
MacVicar

Scarista

Donald
Morrison

Mission
House

To Rodel

Gate Cottage

Bone House

George
Macleod

Dolly
Macleod

Round Garden

Alistair
MacLennan

Scarista
sheep Fank

Old
Golf
Course

ove Lodge

Danny
MacVicar

John
MacDonald

Dolly
Macleod

Poultry house

Sta
bay

Sea shore

SKETCH MAP

Bulaval
353m

E

N

Strath

Maclennan's croft

BORVEBEG
GRAZ

Borve burn

Sitka spruce
Douglas fir

Borve Loch

Heather

Sit
Doug
A:

HORGABOST
COMMON GRAZING

Pinus

Hst.

Rhododendron
ponticum

Peat Bog

Pinus
contorta

THE PARK

MACHAIR

To Tarbert

Loch Cistavat

Sea pool

MACHAIR
THE WARREN

MACHAIR

Estuary

BORVE LODGE
FARM 115 ACRES

Hst = High Spring Tide

Seal ba

SOUND
OF TARANSAY